'Dr Rosina has cleverly [   ]
and stories of leading mii [   ]
knowledge and parenting [   ] to none. This book
represents smart parenting with consciousness and wisdom for the 21st
century. I was delighted to find a powerful and insightful book packed
full of parenting tools and tips from preconception to adolescence. In
fact, this book offers so much I think it is a must read for all, not only
parents!'

*Vivien Sabel, author of the Blossom Method™, UKCP Registered
Psychotherapist, www.viviensabel.com*

'Dr Rosina McAlpine provides parents with a truly inspirational book
to help guide them toward informed appreciation for all that is unique
about their children. With contributions by international experts,
Inspired children helps parents discover their own personal parenting
styles and encourages confidence with actionable ideas that foster
healthy communication, attachment and love. This meaningful book
merges science and experience and, most importantly, it is written in a
language that parents, teachers and early childhood educators can learn
from.'

*Lynne Kenney, PsyD, author of The family coach method,
www.lynnekenney.com*

'This collection of parenting wisdom is focused on the essence of
what mothers and fathers need to know to raise emotionally balanced,
fulfilled and happy children. McAlpine has collated a treasure trove
of guidance from experts who truly care about children's emotional
wellbeing. Parents that are hungry for best-practice parenting ideas
will love Inspired children for its depth of information and its breadth
of subjects ranging from prenatal wellness to developing children's
emotional intelligence.'

Yvette Vignando, publisher of happychild.com.au

'Dr Rosina is passionate about parenting and we all know that to be
successful, children need to have life skills like strong self-esteem,
communication skills and be inspired to achieve great things. This is an

excellent book as it is not just another 'how to' book. All parents can use these methods, ideas and practical suggestions to improve the quality of their relationships with their children and to build their child's self-esteem – which is the cornerstone of every happy, confident child from toddler to teen. Her book is an encouraging and uplifting read for all parents and I recommend you rush out and get your copy now.'

Sue Atkins, author of Raising happy children for dummies, www.TheSueAtkins.com

'I initially assumed that *Inspired children* just another "mommy book" written by women for women. Was I wrong! It is chock full of great ideas for dads. How do you get your kids to help out with the housework? Make it like a game of course! Rosina McAlpine taught her son to sort clothes into different colours and "stuff" them into the washing machine when he was a toddler! Then there is the "bread experiment", an idea so intriguing that every family will want to try it. *Inspired children* is a great read! Not a boring parenting "manual" at all, but a fascinating journey into the hearts and minds of parents and children!'

Charles Areni, professor and single father

'The world needs this incredible book. Dr McAlpine has created an extremely valuable resource filled with the latest research and practical advice to both inform and inspire parents. The concept is unlike any other parenting book. The knowledgeable and caring contributions from these experts will truly have an influence toward … inspired children!'

Deborah McNelis, MSEd, author of the Brain Development Series, www.braininsightsonline.com

'This book is a treasure chest filled with priceless wisdom from many of today's leading-edge thinkers. The rich variety of clear and powerful insights into the inner world of our children will take parents on a journey of understanding that will open their hearts and nurture their soul. Inspired children is a must read for every parent.'

Sandi Schwartz, founder of Leading Edge Parenting, www.sanditeaches.com

Inspired children

How the leading minds of today raise their kids

Edited by Dr Rosina McAlpine

DARLINGTON PRESS

First published by Darlington Press 2011
Darlington Press is an imprint of SYDNEY UNIVERSITY PRESS

Sydney University Press
Fisher Library F03, University of Sydney
NSW 2006 Australia
Email: sup.info@sydney.edu.au

National Library of Australia Cataloguing-in-Publication entry

Title: Inspired children : how the leading minds of today raise
          their kids / edited by Rosina McAlpine.
ISBN: 9781921364181 (pbk.)
Notes: Includes bibliographical references and index.
Subjects: Child rearing.
          Parenting.
          Child development.
Other Authors/Contributors:
          McAlpine, Rosina.
Dewey Number:
          649.1

Cover design by Miguel Yamin, the University Publishing Service
Printed in Australia

For my (beba) Cameron
The inspiration for Inspired children
And sunshine in my life

Contents

Foreword

I believe parenting is one of the most challenging things we will ever do in our lives. I say this for a number of reasons. First, it is a protracted challenge. It is not over quickly. Development through to adulthood occurs over a long time. Second, the non-linear nature of each child's development means not one size fits all at any one point in time, making it difficult to get a concrete grip on the process. As soon as we have got something working with our children, they go and change on us. Third, they change on us differently than their older sibling, or nephew or next door neighbour (and so on), making it difficult to apply strategies that we thought were 'tried and true'. Fourth, the world with which children interact changes. Ongoing technological, environmental and social changes (to name a few) often cut to the heart of the home, leaving parents having to make judgement calls they do not feel equipped to make because they too are struggling to keep up with these changes. Fifth, parents themselves change (as do their circumstances). For example, financial and health concerns will often arise over the long developmental phase and these impact on parenting capabilities and approaches. Sixth, given the imperfect nature of our human condition, it is not unusual for children (or us) to have issues that can threaten or impede the developmental process. For some children this may be a diagnosed disability or specific difficulty (eg with reading). For others it will be a rough patch in their childhood (eg a bout of illness, or bullying, or unhappiness). These things are not easy for parents to deal with. Finally, there is an element of chance, luck and 'randomness' in the whole business – sometimes there are 'bad' days for no identifiable reason, just as there are many great days with no readily identifiable explanation. In all of this, it seems the one thing you can rely on is change.

In my own research program, I have recently built on some of the classic attributes we find are vital to instil in our children – important attributes such as resilience which addresses how children deal with adversity, difficulty and setback. My focus on resilience led to new research looking at 'adaptability', which I define as individuals' capacity to effectively regulate (or adjust) their thoughts, actions, and emotions to deal with changing, uncertain, or novel situations and circumstances. In childhood there are many instances of change and uncertainty: starting school, moving to a new school, moving to a new grade, mastering new school subjects, dealing with a new teacher, adjusting to different teachers, having to get on with new peers, and having to do tasks that are novel or unfamiliar. In fact, these aspects of childhood are so typical that I believe change is more prevalent in our children's lives than is hardship and adversity. To the extent that this is the case, attributes such as adaptability may require at least as much attention in our parenting as resilience.

In many ways, the chapters in this book provide advice on key aspects of adaptability. Collectively, they shed light on children's thinking, behaviour and emotion. They also offer advice on how to attain desirable end states on each of these. There are extensions to children's spiritual lives, which for many parents will be seen as another part of children's adaptability. Indeed, it may be that the joint operation of positive thought, behaviour and emotion represent the fundamentals of *Inspired children*, the title and focus of the book.

The striking feature of this book is the unique bringing together of a number of factors relevant to parenting. It showcases many different parenting approaches and experiences. It illustrates diverse pathways through parenting. It recognises the highs and the lows – and the great bulk of life that resides between these two points. It integrates research with personal anecdotes, experience, professional judgement and practical perspectives. It draws from many disciplines (education to psychology to medicine). It deals with a wide timespan, from preconception to early and middle childhood and then to the teenage years.

As with all parenting publications, the application of this book will vary from parent to parent. These books are not novels where there is a linear passage from start to finish. In reality, different chapters are relevant at different points in the parenting journey. In fact, it is not uncommon for chapters to be read and re-read – with each re-reading feeling like a different chapter because one's needs and experiences have changed since the previous reading.

At a couple of points in the book, authors advise against trying to do everything (or too much) at once. This is good advice and should encourage you to cherry-pick what resonates, what is doable, and what is timely at the point of reading. You do not have to agree on every aspect of the book or chapter within it. With so much advice on offer here, there is something for every parent. On many occasions there will be reassurance – that there are many things parents are doing well. On other occasions there will be insights on how to do things better.

Distilling and synthesising major themes in the book reveals an appreciation of modern parenting life. Headline concepts include the need to address stress, self-esteem (and self-efficacy and confidence), resilience, emotional intelligence, intellectual and emotional stimulation, relationships, money, play, alcohol and other drugs, role modelling, rules and respect. There is also recognition for traditional and non-traditional family structures, including single parents and extended family members such as grandparents.

The authors share quite intimate personal facts and stories. Many also share the typical everyday interactions they have with their own children. The numerous detailed interactions described provide demonstration pieces on how parent–child interactions can be shaped on a day-to-day basis. As noted above, bringing together personal and professional lives is a unique contribution made by this book.

This blend of the personal and professional is also useful because it recognises that parenting need not be a directionless and solely intuitive process. There is good information out there and 'translational' authors (that is, those translating research/professionalism to practice) can provide much needed direction and strategy for a role in life one often feels very ill-equipped to deal with. Drawing on so many authors for different chapters, this book also moves beyond the typical offering of one person's perspective on the whole parenting caper. Again, cherry-picking from this array of advice and practice, parents can develop an approach to parenting tailored to their own needs and aspirations.

Parents make a difference. The impact of their parenting will play out in many ways. Some days will be diamonds and some days will be stones. Sometimes parents' impact will be immediately evident and sometimes there is a 'sleeper' effect such that later that year or well into teenage life it is evident that the message got through. In fact, sometimes it is when the children become parents themselves that you (now a grandparent!) see that the message got through. If you are reading this, it may be that some of the most important steps to be taken have been taken: picking up a book such as this is proof of your mindfulness and good intent as a parent. That is, there is a recognition and awareness that there are options and sliding doors for you to choose. Often each door can lead to positive outcomes – but being aware of others' experiences and expertise can provide greater confidence and peace of mind in making a choice. Sometimes, the door chosen makes a significant difference in a child's life – underscoring the need to be mindful and aware of others' experience and expertise. *Inspired children* is well placed in both respects – laying out diverse journeys, experiences, and expertise upon which parents can draw as their parenting journey unfolds.

I wish you well on your journey.

Andrew Martin

Acknowledgments

There are so many people to thank for their support and effort in making this remarkable book possible.

Colin, my dedicated and loving husband and fabulous father to Cameron, mum Elizabeth, my biggest cheerleader and supporter, and my generous and inspiring sister Dushanka (Dee). Thank you for believing in me and supporting me every step of the way.

I'd also like to acknowledge my gratitude to the amazing authors who have contributed to this book. Thank you for sharing your wisdom with me and, through this book, supporting parents to raise confident, resilient and inspired children. I also wish to say that over the course of writing this book together, you have become very dear to me. A special thank you to Dr Joe Dispenza who agreed to be a contributor when there was only the idea for a book and for his ongoing mentoring and support.

Thank you to Professor Andrew Martin for his wonderful preface which provides his valuable insights into parenting and captures the essence of *Inspired children*.

To the many child development and parenting experts I have met on my journey who are also dear friends now, a heart-felt thank you for being so supportive to the 'newcomer'. Especially, Vivien Sabel, Sue Atkins, Marlaine Cover, and many others.

To my family, friends and colleagues, thank you for all the richness you bring to my life and the many ways you have supported me on this journey.

Finally, to my dear friend and editor at Sydney University Press, Agata, words cannot express how grateful I am for all your support on this book and how much I value our friendship.

Rosina McAlpine

About the authors

Maggie Dent is a well-respected author, educator, and a parenting and resilience expert with a special interest in the early years and adolescence. Her background as a teacher and counsellor has made Maggie a passionate advocate for the healthy, commonsense raising of children in order to strengthen families and communities. She has a broad perspective and range of experience that shapes her work, a slightly irreverent sense of humour and a depth of knowledge that she shares passionately. Her finest achievements are her four sons, deep human connectedness and her many books: *Saving our adolescents* (2010), *Real kids in an unreal world* (2008), *Nurturing kids' hearts and souls* (2005), *Saving our children from our chaotic world* (2010) and *Black duck wisdom* (2004). For more on Maggie Dent and her work, see: www.maggiedent.com.

Dr Joe Dispenza is doctor of chiropractic with training in neurology, neuroscience, brain function and chemistry, cellular biology, memory formation, and aging and longevity. Over the last 10 years, Dr Dispenza has lectured in over 24 different countries on six continents educating people about the role and function of the human brain. He has taught thousands of people how to re-program their thinking through scientifically proven neuro-physiologic principles. His approach, taught in a very simple method, creates a bridge between true human potential and the latest scientific theories of neuroplasticity. He explains how thinking in new ways, as well as changing beliefs, can literally rewire one's brain. The premise of his work is founded in his total conviction that every person on this planet has within them, the latent potential of greatness and true unlimited abilities. His new book, *Evolve your brain: the science of changing your mind* connects the subjects of thought and consciousness with the brain, the mind, and the body. For more information on Dr Dispenza and his work, see: www.drjoedispenza.com.

Sandy Forster is an international speaker, mentor, bestselling author and award-winning business owner. In 2010 Sandy was awarded Australian Home-Based Business of the Year and Overall Company of the Year in the International Awards for Women in Business (New York) and in 2008 International Mentor of the Year. Sandy has transformed her life from welfare to millionaire based on her avid research on the subject of money, prosperity and abundance. She loves mentoring others to create their own success and is the author of six internationally bestselling books, including *How to be wildly wealthy fast* (2004). For more on Sandy Forster and her work, see: www.wildlywealthy.com.

L. Michael Hall, PhD, is a visionary leader in the field of neuro-semantics, self-actualisation psychology and neuro-lingustistic programming (NLP). He has a doctorate in the cognitive-behavioural sciences and works as an entrepreneur, researcher/modeller, and international trainer in NLP. Michael had a therapy practice in Colorado for 15 years, found NLP (1986), created the field of neuro-semantics and later, with Bob Bodenhamer, the International Society of Neuro-Semantics. A prolific writer, Michael has written more than 40 books, including many bestsellers in the field of NLP. Michael first applied NLP to coaching in 1991, and then created meta-coaching with Michelle Duval in 2002 (www.meta-coaching.org).

Bruce H. Lipton, PhD, a cellular and developmental biologist, was formerly Associate Professor of Anatomy at the University of Wisconsin's School of Medicine and a Research Fellow of the School of Medicine at Stanford University. In recognition of his contributions to the fields of embryology and human development, the Association of Prenatal and Perinatal Psychology and Health elected Dr Lipton to their Board of Directors. Bruce has taken his award-winning medical school lectures to the public and is currently a popular keynote speaker and workshop presenter on topics of conscious parenting and the science of complementary medicine. He has published numerous academic research papers and books. To learn more of Dr Lipton, see: www.brucelipton.com.

Professor Andrew Martin is Professorial Research Fellow at the University of Sydney specialising in student motivation, engagement and achievement. He is also a registered psychologist and Honorary Senior Research Fellow in the Department of Education, University of Oxford. He is author of books for parents, *How to motivate your child for school and beyond* (2003) and for teachers, *Building classroom success: eliminating academic fear and failure* (2010), both available at www.lifelongachievement.com.

Dr Rosina McAlpine is an associate professor at the University of Sydney Business School and an internationally recognised teacher and researcher in higher education. She has taught at university for over 20 years and has received four teaching awards and five international best paper awards for her research. Rosina has completed studies in life coaching and neuro linguistic programming (NLP) and has been working as a family life coach for over five years. Since becoming a mother in 2007, her research focus has expanded to include child development and parenting. Drawing on her many years of teaching experience and research into learning she has been able to develop practical and innovative approaches to parenting. She is the founding director of Inspired Children Pty Ltd and the developer of the Inspired Children program. For more on Rosina and her program see: www.inspiredchildren.com.

Jan Roberts has spent more than 40 years in the health care industry, 25 of those working in the area of women's reproductive health. She is a pharmacist with a postgraduate diploma in clinical nutrition and the Australian representative for Foresight, the UK Association for the Promotion of Preconceptual Care. As a co-author of international best-selling series on pregnancy, breastfeeding and babies, Jan has presented preconception workshops and seminars to the general public and health professionals around Australia, NZ and the US since 1987. She has made frequent appearances on radio and TV and is a regular contributor to various magazines and journals. For more information on Jan and her work, see: www.flurishh.com.

Dr Monique Robinson is an Australian Rotary Health Post Doctoral Research Fellow and a registered clinical psychologist working in the field of child and adolescent mental health at the University of Western Australia. Monique's primary research focus has been on the antenatal determinants of behavioural development throughout childhood and adolescence, including stress, hypertension, alcohol and cigarette smoking. This research is based at the Telethon Institute for Child Health Research (www.childhealthresearch.com.au), where longitudinal follow-up continues on a prospective pregnancy cohort. Within the last three years Monique has published numerous journal articles, book chapter and reports, and presented her work at various international meetings. She has been the recipient of 14 early-career researcher awards to date.

Dr Yvonne Sum transforms leaders of tomorrow … today. Through her experience as a dentist, RAAF officer, executive coach, leadership facilitator and speaker, business partner, wife and mother of two, Yvonne has honed her gift of helping others clarify useful behavioural frameworks across various contexts so that we may choose to easily deploy them in our daily lives. She consistently provokes senior business leaders to 'lose their minds and come to their senses' by integrating their leadership insights at home successfully back into the work tribe. Yvonne's breadth of international experience and clientele span across Australia, Asia Pacific and the US. She has presented alongside Edward de Bono, Howard Gardner, Tony Buzan, David Perkins, Glenn Capelli and Colin James. 'Start kidding yourself – learning leadership from your home tribe' is her first book due out in 2012. For more information on Yvonne Sum and her work, see: www.dryvonnesum.com.

Introduction

If you ask any parent the question 'what is the most important thing in your life?' They will inevitably say 'my kids'. And, as a parent, this is true for me too. Since the birth of our son Cameron, I've been buying the 'latest' and 'most popular' books on parenting to inform the many decisions I need to make as a parent, including:

- how long to breastfeed for
- when to introduce solids and in what order
- controlled crying or co-sleeping
- immunise (homeopathic or pharmaceutical) or not to immunise
- go back to work (full time/part time) and how to manage child care
- how to support Cameron's development for achieving the key 'milestones'
- how to manage toddler tantrums
- the best ways to discipline, to support self-esteem and to develop key life skills.

And the list goes on.

Parents have to make so many important decisions, ones that may affect their child for the rest of their life. So, as a parent I want to get it right. While there are many good books with helpful information available, to my disappointment, I also found that parenting books provide conflicting advice and are filled with authors 'opinions' rather than research into child development and parenting.

When I asked other parents for their advice I received comments like 'just use your intuition, common sense, trial and error and learn as you go'. That was of little comfort to me. It made me think about how society as a whole seems to view parenting as something you can do just because you can have a child. This assumption is pervasive even across cultures. However, in reality, parenting is the most important and most complicated job in the world if you view it in terms of looking after the emotional, physical, psychological and cognitive development of another human being. Today, to be a parent, we require no experience, qualifications or training, yet most jobs we do in life – chef, builder, accountant, doctor or actor to name but a few, require some kind of experience, education and/or training. When you think about parenting in this way it's a very curious assumption, isn't it?

Perhaps we wouldn't need to question or to change our model of parenting if there was evidence that we are currently doing a good job and that just 'winging it' is actually working.[1] And while it is so important to acknowledge that parents do the best they can and there are many happy and healthy children, sadly, the statistics reveal that this is not true for all children and families.

We have a problem right now! An increasing number of children are depressed, obese, lack basic life skills, abuse drugs and alcohol, have behavioural problems such as attention deficit hyperactivity disorder (ADHD), engage in destructive behaviours and, tragically, even commit suicide. It is clear that many children of today need more guidance to help them lead a functional life at the minimum and preferably an inspired and successful life.

Parents want the best for their children, but the fast and demanding pace of life has left them time poor and stressed. They don't have the time to research the latest findings in child development, unless they come up against a behavioural, physical, cognitive or emotional problem and they need help to manage it. Perhaps many of these problems could be avoided, rather than managed, if parents were more proactive and had practical resources to help them understand how to support their child's development. In order to achieve this, parents need some practical guidance over and above what the standard parenting books offer.

Wouldn't it be so much easier for parents if they could make their most important decisions based on scientific evidence rather than

---

1 'Winging it' refers to jumping in and doing something without preparation and hoping it will be OK.

people's opinions? Wouldn't we have better outcomes for children if parents based their parenting approaches on tried and tested methods rather than by trial and error? This is how I want to parent, and so for almost four years now, I've been researching and working with experts to find out the latest research into child development and parenting. My aim is to turn the science of child development into the art of parenting and to share it with other parents.

Please understand that I don't believe parenting is all about information and science. For me, love, connection, presence, intuition and the human spirit are at the heart of parenting and these are present in my every day interactions with our son Cameron. My approach to parenting is to blend all I have within myself with the latest research to inform my decisions and actions. As you read on, you'll see that the experts who have contributed to this wonderful book also value a holistic approach to parenting and integrate science, love, personal experience and the human spirit in their approaches.

This book provides a practical guide to raising children from preconception to teenage years. It includes areas of interest for parents-to-be, including how to prepare for conception in order to give a child the best start in life and ways to avoid stress during pregnancy and its negative effects on the unborn child. Parents, grandparents and teachers can learn how to support a child's development in fundamental areas like good self-esteem, resilience and managing emotions and behaviour. Practical activities and guidance are provided on how children can develop skills in setting and achieving goals, communicating, building and nurturing relationships with family and friends, managing stress, understanding health and nutrition as well as environmental awareness and social consciousness. These key life skills and personal qualities are the platform from which a child can create a happy, productive and fulfilling life. Parents are also introduced to a framework for managing their family life and making it all work.

Readers will find *Inspired children* unique as it is not based on the philosophies or views of one or two authors, but on the research, experience and expertise of a number of thought leaders of our times. Contributors in this book are experts in their respective fields including personal development, psychology, biology, genetics and child development among others. The authors share how they have used their expert knowledge to successfully raise their own children. While the chapters are based on the latest research, they are written in an easy to understand and practical way, and include numerous personal examples from the contributors about their approaches to, and the challenges they experienced, raising their own children.

Each of the authors has made a significant contribution to our current understanding of how we can improve our lives, our children's lives and the planet. For example, Bruce H. Lipton received the 2009 Goi Peace Award in recognition of his pioneering work in the field of 'new biology'. His personal mission is to spread the important message of his research findings – that each individual is a powerful creator of their personal life and the world they live in. His books and seminars help individuals to understand the complexities of life and to live the best life possible.

Other authors in this book have also made significant contributions through publishing research (e.g. Robinson et al. 2008 and 2011), participating in films (e.g. *What the bleep do we know!?, What the bleep!? Down the rabbit hole* and *The secret*), authoring books (e.g. *Evolve your brain* by Joe Dispenza, *Spontaneous evolution* by Bruce H. Lipton and Steve Bhaerman, and *The natural way to better babies* by Francesca Naish and Janette Roberts), and developing programs and presenting seminars (e.g. The Inspired Children program and The 7Rs of Good Parenting).

Many adults seek to understand and improve their lives through personal development programs and books. This is evident by the huge personal development market. It is possible, however, to start this journey as children if parents are given the right guidance. It is easy to imagine that the world would be a far better place if parents were able to help children understand that they are powerful creators of their life and have the potential to impact the world in a positive way.

My journey into parenthood

I met Colin, the love of my life, when I was 42 years old. By February of the following year we were pregnant and in May we were married on Observatory Hill in Sydney in the most intimate, beautiful wedding you can imagine. Our life was wonderful, we were newlyweds and we were so excited about becoming parents. Together we did as much reading and preparation as we could to ensure we got it right with our first child!

I knew how important it was to eat well, rest, exercise and stay as calm and centred as I could during my pregnancy to give our beba[2] the best chance in life. Whenever I felt tired I made sure I took the time to rest and I imagined that I was making my beba's eyebrows, or my beba's toes and that of course was more important than any deadline I had to meet, cleaning I had to do or meeting I should attend. Imagining how our beba was growing inside me made it important, as well as fun, to rest. I read many books on pregnancy and birth both before and during my pregnancy. I couldn't get enough information and I couldn't wait to meet my beba – to hold, to cuddle and to kiss him, but I didn't look beyond that.

On 22 November 2007, at 10:33 pm I became a mother. It was the most amazing moment in time and changed the course of my life forever.

I never really thought much about what it means to be responsible for the life of another being until our beautiful Cameron came home from hospital and I had to take care of him every day. The first few months of our life together are a bit of a blur – all I can remember is being absolutely enamoured with him and often just staring at him for hours. Like most new mothers I was sleep deprived and relied on my wonderful husband Colin, my mother and sister to help me make the huge adjustment from full-time work to full-time motherhood.

My new life had many ups and some downs too. Apart from the joy of taking care of Cameron, there were the day-to-day activities like cleaning the house and earning income. In the early days, I often felt

---

2 Beba is baby in Serbian, and it was and still is our name for Cameron – he's our beba Cameron – the baby of the family.

totally incompetent and overwhelmed with emotion. I couldn't believe how much I'd changed and how I could go from managing a very successful and demanding university career to feeling overwhelmed! Most new parents can probably relate the huge life changes I experienced during those first few months.

Some months later, I started to come back in touch with reality and found a new routine for my life. It was only then that the exciting and daunting task I had ahead became clear to me. I felt the enormous responsibility I had taken on in deciding to co-parent a child, and I had no idea how I was going to do it.

Like all parents I want the best for our child, but I realised very quickly that I didn't have the skills to take care of him in the way I wished to. I realised that a child is such a complex being and I didn't have a clue how to support his life. What did I know about cognitive, emotional, physical and psychological development – just to name some of the main areas? How was I going to be able to nurture and support Cameron to give him the best chance at reaching his potential and living a happy and fulfilling life?

As I explained in the opening paragraphs, I found many good parenting books which were helpful for the day-to-day issues parents face when raising children. I found useful information on food, play and developmental milestones. I also found, however, that depending on which author I read, there were slight differences or sometimes completely opposing recommendations as to what was the right thing to do. Co-sleeping versus separate cots, no solids until six months versus solids at four months, immunisation is safe versus immunisation is harmful, to name just a few of the contradictory positions. I found this very frustrating because I wanted to make sure I got it right. I needed to know the best approach! I'm not saying I needed to be perfect, that wasn't the challenge I set myself, but I wanted to be a competent and good mother.[3]

I also wanted to know how to support Cameron's development in all key aspects of his life. How was I going to support him to acquire a

---

3 Some people refer to this perspective as the 'good-enough parent'. See for example Bettelheim 1987.

strong sense of self and become resilient? What would I need to do to help him manage his emotions and develop good communication skills, leadership qualities, and to be able to nurture strong relationships with his family and friends? In what ways could I help him become aware of how he can make a positive impact on society and the environment? How would I help him discover the purpose of his life and ways to lead a happy and fulfilling life? How was I going to help him develop all of these essential life skills and be an *inspired child*?

Phew! Thank goodness I decided that I had some time to learn about all of these things as he was only a baby and so I could, little by little, do the research and find the answers to these questions for our Cameron.

I've been an educator over 20 years and my expertise is in teaching and learning. I have a Master's degree and a PhD in education and so I knew I could use my skills to learn everything I needed to know about how to be a good parent. I thought a good place to start would be to determine the key life skills I would like to help Cameron develop.

My research revealed that children need to develop many fundamental life skills to lead a fulfilling and successful life. I came up with this list of skills and personal qualities:

- a strong sense of self and resilience
- an understanding the importance of maintaining a healthy body
- the ability to manage emotions and behaviours
- good communication and relationship-building skills
- the motivation and ability to learn and grow as a person
- the desire to interact with the natural environment and society in a positive way
- the ability to relax and have fun
- the inspiration to live a meaningful, happy and productive life.

I then classified these skills into seven broad categories namely: personal power (self-esteem and resilience); health and wellbeing; education, career and money; social and environmental understanding;

communication skills and relationships; relaxation and play; as well as inspired creativity. The next step was to develop different activities under each of the headings so Cameron could over time, in a systematic rather than haphazard way, develop key life skills necessary for an inspired life. Then I began my research on these key topics. I found lots of resources on the internet, books, journals and courses that were relevant to one or a few key life skills areas. What I couldn't find was a single resource that comprehensively dealt with all of the life skills at an affordable price. By now you've probably noticed I chose to take a thorough, step-by-step, research-based educational approach to this whole process.

I loved doing the research and learning. The knowledge and skills made me feel much more confident about being a good mum. I felt so inspired and excited about the project that I had to share it with my friends and family to gather their wisdom and experience as well. The more I spoke with others about what I was working on, the more it became apparent that other parents wanted and needed help too. I remember my family, friends and the mums in my mother's group saying, you can't keep this to yourself, you need to share it with everyone. I knew this was true even though I had no idea how I was going to make this happen. One night as I was pondering on it, I came up with the name Inspired Children. I knew it was fate that the program would become a reality when I was able to buy the domain name www.inspiredchildren.com and the business name was available. These were my signs and the Inspired Children program was conceived!

The life skills and personal qualities listed above became my working definition of what an inspired child would be like. Over the last few years, I've developed an easy to use and affordable program which takes very little time to complete to suit the lifestyles of busy parents and children. Most importantly, the program is based on the latest research and knowledge about child development as well as commonsense life skills. The Inspired Children program provides guidance and resources to empower parents help their children develop key life skills across the seven areas in only 15 minutes at a time.

Alongside developing the Inspired Children program I decided to put this book together. Its title, *Inspired children: how the leading minds of today raise their kids,* became the obvious choice after I'd interviewed these amazing contributors. How this book came about is a story in itself.

Since my early 20s, I've been interested in personal development and, to this end, I have attended many seminars and read a large number of books on the topic. One such seminar, given by Dr Joe Dispenza on The Science of Changing Your Mind, was the inspiration for this book. Dispenza spoke about how he helped his children develop emotional intelligence and other key life skills. I was transfixed on hearing his words and I realised that there are people out there like him who have the knowledge, expertise and most importantly the experience of raising children in a supportive environment so their kids could live an inspired life. I knew I had to find these people!

After his seminar, I spoke with him about my inspired children project and the book on child development. To my delight, he not only graciously agreed to contribute to the book, he suggested that I invite his good friend and co-presenter Bruce H. Lipton to participate. Dispenza explained that a child's development begins well before the child is conceived and Lipton could tell me all about it. You can imagine my shock at hearing that a child's development begins *before* it is conceived? How does that make sense? I guessed that I would find out soon enough and I certainly did! Once these first few chapters started to take shape it didn't take long to find the remaining contributors for this extraordinary book.

I can't tell you how amazing each of these authors are and how generous they have been with their time and knowledge. They have shared many incredible insights into raising children based on the latest research and their own personal experiences. This book is the result of my perseverance and their hard work and generosity of spirit. The knowledge I've gained has changed my life – I've learned so much and can't wait to share it with you. Here is a taste of what's to come.

About the book

The story of our journey into understanding a child's development begins in the first chapter on preconception. Bruce H. Lipton, PhD shares his insights into how parents can influence their child's physical, emotional and intellectual development even before a baby is conceived. I know this may sound implausible; however, you will see how it works once you've read his easy to follow explanations on the recent scientific discoveries in the field of epigenetics. Lipton explains how parents can give their child the best possible start in life. He also informs parents which lifestyle choices to avoid, providing research which shows that they can harm a child's development.

Dr Monique Robinson's chapter continues the story as she discusses the effects of stress during pregnancy on the unborn child. Her research shows that stress in pregnancy can lead to behavioural or emotional problems in babies which can extend, not only into childhood, but right up into adolescent years. Robinson reveals the link between the increasing levels of stress in society and the increasing numbers of children developing attention deficit and other such disorders. Imagine how helpful it would be for pregnant women to know the findings of this research. Being informed would mean a mother could choose to takes steps to reduce her stress levels for the duration of the pregnancy – knowing that this could make a lifetime of difference for her unborn child. Being informed would also mean that as a society, we could choose to support pregnant women and their unborn children whenever possible.

Once the child is born there is much to know about raising a healthy and happy baby. In chapter three, Jan Roberts shows parents how to work with their inner wisdom and integrate this with the latest research and knowledge on raising babies. She explores many key areas including: breastfeeding, sleeping, stress, parental instincts and ways to support the cognitive and emotional development of your baby. Parents will gain insights into the benefits of prolonged breastfeeding, co-sleeping and appropriate stimulation for the physical, intellectual and emotional wellbeing of babies.

In the fourth chapter, written by me, Dr Rosina McAlpine, I discuss how parents can prepare children for life by helping them to develop key life skills and personal qualities including good self-esteem, resilience, emotional intelligence and a social conscience. The seven key life skill areas I described earlier are explored. Practical activities provide parents, grandparents, carers and teachers with the resources and the knowhow to help children develop key life skills and personal qualities that will support them to lead successful and fulfilling lives.

In chapter five, Dr Joe Dispenza explains how to nurture the emotional development of children to help them learn how to behave in a way that is supportive to them and to others. Wouldn't it be wonderful if your child could manage their emotions and their behaviours in a positive way? Throughout the chapter Dispenza provides many examples and activities he has practised with his children which have helped them to become resourceful and responsive young adults.

Good self-esteem is a valuable personal quality in life. I can't imagine any parent wanting their child to have poor self-esteem, yet this is true for many children of today. In chapter six, Michael L. Hall, PhD explains the fundamental differences between self-esteem, self-confidence and self-efficacy and shows parents why it is important to understand these differences in order to raise psychologically healthy children. He provides practical ways to nurture good self-esteem in children so they can interact with life in a confident and positive way.

We live in a fast-paced, stressful world. In chapter seven, Maggie Dent explains that many adults can't manage their stress because they didn't learn how to deal with stress and distress as children. Given we know that most illnesses are stress related, it is crucial that parents, carers and educators equip children with the tools to calm themselves and be able to manage stress. Drawing on her research and experience of raising four boys, Dent provides guidance and helpful suggestions on how to achieve this. She also touches on the topics parents never want to associate with their own children – drugs, alcohol and violence, and explains how to engage children in safe activities like athletics and creative pursuits.

In an interview with Dr Joe Dispenza, I discovered how he helped his children to develop a positive relationship with life. In chapter eight parents learn about a number of simple and fun activities the family can complete together to create opportunities for children to experience for themselves how they can influence the world and therefore feel motivated to take responsibility for leading an inspired life.

Realising dreams and achieving life goals makes for a successful and joyful life. In chapter nine, Sandy Forster shares her insights into the process of making dreams a reality by role modelling and involving your children. Parents can discover how to help children focus on what they want to achieve and take the steps towards making it happen. Forster inspires the reader with her own amazing story of how she went from being on welfare to becoming a millionaire.

Busy parents trying to manage a career, run a household, parent and find time for themselves will find the final chapter helpful. Dr Yvonne Sum explains her 7Rs of Parenting framework which helps parents bring order and structure to family life. Parenting processes include role modelling, having rules, engendering respect, developing routines as well as making time for reviewing, reflecting and reorganising when needed!

Every chapter is filled with helpful information, practical activities you can complete with your children as well as many personal and heart-warming accounts the contributors share about their parenting and their children. I was so fortunate to have the opportunity to interview many of their children. I wanted to hear about their children's experiences of being parented. You know, to me the proof of the pudding is in the eating and I wanted a taste of what was possible for children with inspired parents.

During our conversations I was moved to tears many times as they shared their wonderful childhood experiences. Here are some of the highlights:

> I never understood why my friends had to lie to their parents about what they were doing or where they were going. Mum and I always talked about everything.

> Everyday dad asked us the same question. 'Are you happy? If not why not and what are you going to do about it.' I still ask myself that question and live my life that way today.

I didn't feel the need to be popular or to do things because of peer pressure. I knew what was right from wrong – I knew it inside.

Breastfeeding is so natural I can't understand why some people have a problem with mothers feeding their babies in public.

When we did things with dad we always left the people and things in a better way than we found them. That made a big impression on me and I now have a career doing that.

Most of all I always felt loved and valued as a person in my own right.

They truly are inspired children and I'll be so happy if our Cameron grows up with such fine personal qualities, attitudes and life skills. I hope one day to share more of the insights I gained from these inspired children – but that's another book!

I don't really know why as a society we have believed for so long that we don't we need help with parenting and that we can parent without any research, knowledge and skills. As soon as I started to learn more I felt so empowered – I felt like I knew what I was doing and most importantly why I was doing it.

This book is a guide for parents who want to raise an inspired child. I hope you find reading this book as interesting and empowering as I did creating it.

My sincere and heart-felt best wishes on your parenting journey.

Dr Rosina McAlpine

Further readings and resources

Bettelheim B (1987). *A good enough parent: the guide to bringing up children.* London: Thames and Hudson Ltd.

Dispenza J (2007). *Evolve your brain: the science of changing your mind.* Deerfield Beach, Florida: Health Communications Inc.

Lipton BH & Bhaerman S (2010). *Spontaneous evolution: our positive future (and a way to get there from here).* Hay House Inc.

Naish F & Roberts J (1996). *The natural way to better babies: preconception healthcare for prospective parents.* Sydney: Random House.

Robinson M, Mattes E, Oddy WH, Pennell CE, van Eekelen JAM, McLean NJ, Jacoby P, Li J, de Klerk NH, Zubrick SR, Stanley FJ & Newnham JP (2011). Prenatal stress events and behavioural development from age two to 14 years: the influence of the number, type and timing of stressful life experiences. *Development and Psychopathology,* 23(2): 507–20.

Robinson M, Oddy WH, Li J, Kendall GE, de Klerk NH, Silburn S, Zubrick SR, Newnham JP, Stanley FJ & Mattes E (2008). Pre- and postnatal influences on preschool mental health: a large-scale cohort study. *Journal of Child Psychology & Psychiatry,* 49(10): 1118–28.

The Inspired Children program. Available: www.inspiredchildren.com/

The secret (2006). Film directed by D Heriot. Melbourne: Prime Time Productions.

The 7Rs of Good Parenting. Available: www.dryvonnesum.com/Product/The-7Rs-of-Parenting.html.

What the bleep do we know!? (2004). Film directed by W Arntz, B Chasse & M Vicente.

What the bleep!? Down the rabbit hole (2006). Film directed by W Arntz, B Chasse & M Vicente.

1

Preparing for parenthood

Bruce H. Lipton, PhD

Most parenting books focus on child development after the baby is born. While many pregnancy books acknowledge that there are general benefits if mothers and fathers interact with their unborn child by reading, talking, singing and playing music – very little is explained about how crucial pregnancy is in child development. What appears to be missing from the general parenting books of today is that raising a child begins well before the child is even conceived. It is not common knowledge that preparations for conception as well as a mother's experience during pregnancy play a significant part in providing a strong foundation for raising an inspired child.

This chapter is relevant to prospective parents as well as parents. Parents-to-be can learn about some of the key issues they need to consider when preparing for conception and parenthood. Parents can understand more about how their lifestyle choices prior to conception and their current actions as a parent can significantly impact their child in either a positive or negative way. The most important point is to recognise that knowledge and understanding is power. Without knowledge and understanding people act from ignorance and subsequently have to deal with the consequences of their actions. The advantage is that once a person *understands* about the consequences of their actions, they are in a position of strength as they can make *informed* choices. This chapter provides numerous insights into preparing for parenting. Given parenting can be the most rewarding as well as the most challenging activity in life, the more knowledge we have, the more we are empowered to take actions that are more likely to lead to positive outcomes in our own life and the life of our child.

From generation to generation

It is within our nature for each generation to strive to do things better than the last. This is the nature of evolution. The same can be said about parenting. Before the birth of their own children, how many times have you heard a person say: 'when I have kids I will never be like my parents' or 'I will never treat my child the way my parents treated me' or 'I'll be so much more understanding and supportive with my children than my parents were with me'? As a prospective parent, perhaps you feel like this too.

If you already have a child, and if you are really honest with yourself, you might be able to admit that you have said similar things, only to find that after your child was born, you caught yourself saying and doing exactly what your parents said and did even though you were so determined not to!

How does this happen?

When we first become parents, generally all we really know about parenting is the model handed down to us by our own parents – good or bad. Regardless of whether we feel we had a good, bad or somewhere in between parenting experience, we can choose to accept that our parents did the best they could with the level of knowledge, understanding and skills they had in relation to parenting. We also need to accept that how well we were parented determines the basic level of skill that we start out with as parents ourselves. So, unless at some time we have made a conscious effort to learn a new model of parenting and have been successful in putting the new model into action, our experience of being parented is how we subsequently parent. This happens despite our best intentions.

Why does this happen?

While there is no simple answer to this complex issue, one important part of the story begins after we are born. You may have heard many child development experts say that until the age of about six or seven, children are like sponges. They absorb everything uncensored from their environment including their experience of parenting. These parenting experiences become recorded or programmed in their subconscious only to be retrieved and replayed subconsciously in the future once they have their own children.

Subconsciously?

While we would all like to think that we lead our lives consciously rather than based on subconscious programs, on average we actually only spend about 5% of our day consciously. Think about it. How much of the day are you actually consciously aware and present to what you are doing? Let's get more specific to make the point. How many times have you walked or driven from one place to another on autopilot? How many times have you asked yourself if you locked the front door or turned off the iron because you weren't really 'there' – conscious and present when you were leaving home or ironing? Are you beginning to see how much of your day is not conscious? Better still – try this exercise. Make a conscious decision to stay present (conscious) as long as you can from the time you awake and get out of bed tomorrow morning or from the time you leave from your home. Remember, this involves being continually aware and present to yourself and your environment, and not going into your mind thinking about in the future or the past. See how long you last or see if you even remember!

While most people operate using subconscious programs for about 95% of their day, it is important to know that automatic programs are not bad in themselves – in fact they are essential to help us function efficiently in the world. However, if the subconscious programs have negative impacts on us personally or others in our lives such as our children, this is where these programs can be harmful and need to be addressed.

So back to parenting, if we accept that 95% of our day is spent using subconscious programs, and that we have many programs that will not be supportive for raising our child, how do we prepare to become parents?

The good news is that conscious parenting is a skill that everyone can learn like any other – only if a person has an interest in acquiring new knowledge and has the ability to put the new knowledge into practice. However, achieving this on your own is hard, given we generally can't see our own subconscious programs. The most effective way then, is to find a supportive partner to co-parent with you and help you on the journey!

While most individuals have the intention to co-parent before they become parents, sometimes things don't work out and they both end up as single parents and this was true in my case. My wife and I separated when my children were ten and seven years old and we both continued to parent our girls while living apart. The concept of a parenting partner is still relevant for single parenting. The key is that when single parents are with their child, they have supportive people in their life to help them see and work with their subconscious parenting programs. It is also crucial for a single parent to be as self-reflective as possible and in a sense be their own parenting partner! A life partner, friend or relative can be a supportive parenting partner – the main thing is that they are around regularly when the single parent is parenting and can support them in the right way.

The supportive parenting partner

Ideally, a parenting partner is actively co-parenting with you, but where this is not possible, the principles described below can be applied to other parenting partners. What a 'supportive parenting partner' is will, of course, be different for each person. However, to become a conscious parent, to uncover and disengage potentially harmful automatic subconscious programs and to develop new supportive subconscious parenting programs, is most achievable with a parenting partner – people who can work together at a deep level. This is fundamental for creating a supportive environment in which to raise an inspired child.

The nature of our subconscious programs is that we don't see them when they are playing out – they are called subconscious programs as they play out below or outside our consciousness. So while a parent has the intention and desire to parent consciously, the subconscious programs automatically come in when we are not consciously aware, which is about 95% of the time. While we can't generally see our subconscious for ourselves, other people can. This is how a supportive parenting partner can help. Imagine if two people came together with the understanding that they will help each other uncover and transform harmful subconscious programs not just in relation to parenting but in relation to everything. This would create an ideal environment for personal growth for everyone – the adults as well as the child.

How do supportive parenting partnerships work?

The best way to explain why parenting partnerships are so crucial for good parenting and to illustrate how parenting partnerships work, is to provide examples of supportive parenting partnerships in action. If one parent, let's call them 'parent-A', is interacting with a child and is enacting harmful subconscious parenting programs, it is the job of the observing parenting partner to point this out. That is, to bring it to the attention of parent-A's consciousness. For this to work, each person in the parenting partnership needs to have previously agreed to this and developed a variety supportive ways to do this – ways which will help parent-A accept and reflect on the automatic behaviour as opposed to react and defend themselves. Once parent-A is made aware of their subconscious program, this awareness could then give rise to a variety of positive actions by parent-A which will vary from person to person and situation to situation.

For example, a positive response and course of action for parent-A could be to leave the room in order to have some space to calm, reflect and return when they are able to act more consciously. The other parent can then take over interacting with the child and explain with words to the effect of:

> everything is fine, mummy (or daddy) just needs a little time to think about the things they have just said and done and we will talk more about it with you soon.

Upon the return of parent-A, it is important to provide an age-appropriate explanation of what is happening in relation to parent-A, so that the child can understand what is going on in their world. In this way parent-A is both explaining to the child the process of uncovering and transforming subconscious programming as well as modelling personal development and growth for their child.

Another option could be for parent-A to say to the parenting partner 'thanks for pointing that out' and then openly exploring what was unveiled with the parenting partner and the child – only if they are in the right frame of mind and calm enough to do this. Again, it is really important to provide an age-appropriate explanation of what is happening for the child to help them understand and learn from the experience.

In my own parenting, I can recall times when I was not in a good mood as the result of a bad day, my subconscious programs were running and I was short with or shouted at my child. Once I calmed down I would apologise and then explain that I was angry because of what had happened during my day and that I was not upset with them. I would take the time to reassure my child that my outburst had nothing to do with them!

I also used these situations as broader learning opportunities for my children. For example, I explained how this kind of situation may happen many times in their life, because at one time or another, everyone (adults and children) gets angry, sad or reacts negatively at other people, and it will generally have nothing to do with the person they are reacting to. They may just have a lot going on inside. I also explored possible courses of action my child could take if this happened to them again.

For example, I would guide them and suggest that in these situations, it is best to remain calm and that they can experiment with different ways to respond. We talked about how they might simply acknowledge the person's feelings and offer support or offer space with a sentence like 'I can see you are upset, is there something I can do to help or would you like to be alone?' The conversations that followed allowed my children and me to explore a variety of scenarios and outcomes through discussion and role-playing. This gave my children an understanding of these kinds of situations and some options for dealing with them, if and when they happen. Further, my children understood that they did not need to take on feelings of guilt for other people's bad day, while still taking responsibility for their own actions and being reflective of the situation to see the part they played in the situation.

It was also important to point out to my children that they too have subconscious programs and that they will act using them from time to time and that some of these actions may have a negative impact on others. My children, like everyone else's, will have times when they get angry or terse with a friend or relative. It is important to discuss the consequences of the various ways this might play out. The important thing is to make it real, fun and interesting. For example, you can invite your child to be a scientist and uncover automatic reactions that they generally don't see, identify those that are not working so well in their life, and learn how to change them. Also as a parent, it is important to help your child become aware of their subconscious programs and ways to transform them.

Coming back to parenting partnerships and reflecting on the positive exchange provided between parent-A and their parenting partner, shows how helpful it can be for a child to have parents in a supportive parenting partnership. It is easy to see that an important part of preparing to become a parent is to find a supportive parenting partner which will then allow each partner to explore their own subconscious negative programs and create new supportive programs. This partnership allows for personal growth and for a continual improvement in the home environment for the child. More importantly it provides a powerful model for the child – the model that will be recorded into their subconscious mind which will be their way of operating in the world. In this case, the child's subconscious programs will reflect the parents positive modelling – that uncovering subconscious programs is a good thing which helps people learn and grow. This model of parenting also creates a space for the parents to explore with their child how the child can work with their own subconscious programs in a supportive way as well as how they operate in others. Many different ways that parents can help their child learn many valuable life skills are discussed in more detail in the later chapters of this book.

While it is easy to see why supportive parenting partners can create the best possible environment for a child, it is important to acknowledge that supportive parenting partnerships are *not* easy to achieve. In fact, it takes a great deal of courage, self-insight and understanding about personal growth to allow another person to help you uncover your negative subconscious programs and then to look at them and transform them. At the end of this chapter, there are a number of references to help those interested in the process of uncovering subconscious programs and make positive life changes.

If we accept that personal discovery and change are difficult, we understand why most people defend, deflect and get very angry when their negative subconscious programs are revealed. You probably find this happens to you too! This is the model of parenting that most children grow up with, so it becomes the model most people use in their adult life. However, the growth of the personal development industry is testament to the fact that some people realise that this is an old model and it is not working for them. When this happens, they search for courses and resources to discover new models. Many courses emphasise how important it is to uncover, accept and transform your subconscious programs to grow in life. It is now becoming clear how valuable it can be to have parents who model discovery and growth rather than parents who model covering up, defensiveness, fear and anger, especially if we remember that it is when we are conscious that we have real choice and for 95% of the time we operate from our subconscious automatic programs. It seems then, that allowing a partner to help us uncover unsupportive automatic programs is a way to get back choice!

It is probably becoming obvious that there are many negative consequences of unsupportive parenting partnerships – where the parenting partners don't allow for the uncovering of subconscious programs, personal growth and change. It is worth exploring some actual examples to make sure this picture is really clear! A child who grows up in a negative environment is more likely to experience parents who are angry, deflect blame and criticise each other and the child is likely to be fearful, feel they are to blame for the conflict, and feel insecure and possibly unloved. This is obviously not a nurturing environment for a child.

Parent-1: 'Johnny, I have told you 100 times be careful with your juice – look you clumsy thing – you have poured juice all over the floor – when will you learn!'

Parent-2: 'Stop yelling at that child ... he's only five. What do you expect? You're just in a bad mood and when you get that way you're just like your dad – angry and impatient. Look at him can you see how scared he is right now?'

Child is crying, scared, listening to all of this conflict as it is being recorded into his subconscious.

Parent-1: 'What would you know? I'm nothing like my father. This is about Johnny – he has to learn to listen and be careful – you're just too soft. Do you think that is going to help him in life if we're too soft? He needs boundaries he needs to know what's right and wrong. You're into this soft new age parenting. You think because you've read a couple of parenting books you're the expert now?'

Parent-2: 'You're impossible to talk to you and you won't look at anything in yourself – everyone else is to blame. I can't do this anymore you're too hard to live with.'

Parents become aware Johnny is listening to all of this.

Parent-1: 'Johnny, go to your room and have some time out and think about what you've done.'

Johnny goes to his room alone, crying, now more scared, blaming himself why do I have to be so clumsy and make mum and dad fight. Listening to all of this conflict, he worries about his parents separating all the while EVERYTHING is being recorded into his subconscious.

Now this might seem an extreme example, but in reality, in our day-to-day life, arguments much like these occur in all families. If you reflect honestly about how you interact with your parenting partner and your child, can you see similar, even if not as extreme, examples in your life? Are you starting to see the consequences of regular negative experiences on your child?

Apart from the obvious negative emotional impact on the child, let's look at the more subtle long-lasting consequences of this type of parenting environment. The subtext of this argument between the parents is being recorded in the child's subconscious mind. This subconscious programming will then be the way that child functions in the world 95% of the time. The subtext is: don't look at your subconscious programs, if your programs are ever uncovered, get angry, deflect the claims with criticism and blame; relationships are not about supporting personal development; defend your position, don't reflect and certainly don't explore alternatives to find a better way; and finally don't include your child in the conversation, don't talk to them about what is actually happening and don't explore how they might be feeling.

Having read the positive and negative impacts parents can have on their child's life, where are you at now? Are you overwhelmed, surprised, angry, depressed, concerned, in denial, feeling guilty or even scared? If you are feeling any of these emotions it is perfectly understandable. However, once you put these feelings aside, what will you do with this new knowledge? While it is true that the negative consequences of unsupportive parenting partnerships can range from unhelpful to horrific effects upon the child depending upon how negative the child's environment is, a little knowledge can go a long way if used correctly. Remember the point we made at the beginning of this chapter? The aim of the chapter is to empower you with knowledge and understanding so you can make informed choices.

If parents realise that the way they model growth and change in their own lives will become the way their child will operate in the world, they can consciously work on providing more supportive models. Imagine how incredibly helpful it would be for any person, if as a child they had a supportive parenting environment and their subconscious beliefs and programs were along the lines of: everyone has unhelpful subconscious programs that they have developed over time; having a partner in life who is willing to work with you to uncover and transform them is a wonderful way to grow and change; if my parenting model is one of openness, striving for growth and change, my child will record this in its subconscious and that will be their way of being in the world. Now this is empowering and the foundation for creating an inspired life!

Where to from here?

That is up to you. If you are currently a parent and have a parenting partner, you may already be working in a supportive way – that is wonderful – keep going. If you see you can make improvements, then you can take this knowledge and act on it to create a new way to parent. Working with a supportive parenting partner is a very helpful way to make a difference in your child's life. The great news is that it is never too late to make change for the better. On the other hand, if you are preparing for parenthood you can now see how valuable, rather, how crucial it is to find a supportive parenting partner. Once you have someone to work with, the next step is to prepare together for the conception of your child.

There is a growing awareness of the importance of maintaining general health and wellbeing before conceiving a child. Simply put, the advice is to eat well, take the recommended nutritional supplements, exercise and avoid poor lifestyle choices like drugs, cigarettes and alcohol. Doing this will give you the best chance for a healthy conception. While this is a crucial part of the process of preparing to conceive, this is not the complete picture!

Most people realise that poor lifestyle choices affect their own health. Most people also believe that poor lifestyle choices *don't* affect their genetics and therefore would not affect the genes they pass on to their child. However, there is growing evidence to suggest that this is, in fact, wrong! Research shows that there is a great deal more in addition to general physical health and wellbeing to consider before conceiving a child. We now have new knowledge and a greater understanding that a person's lifestyle can actually impact their genetics. These research findings arise out of a relatively new and very exciting area of research called epigenetics.

This research has discovered that lifestyle choices can affect a person's genetic *expression* and that a genetic expression can be passed on to a child at conception though its parents' sperm and egg. So it seems that understanding the latest findings of epigenetic research is really important to potential parents, and they need to know this prior to their child's conception. Epigenetics can explain how parents can significantly impact the life of their child in a positive or negative way. While genetics is an extremely complex area, how this works can be simplified to get the main messages across.

There are a number of aspects to consider in relation to genetics. First, there is the *gene* itself. Second is the gene's activity or *expression*. Third, the gene's expression is *received* and subsequently *affects* the body. Some genetic expressions will affect the body in a positive way resulting in good health and longevity, others will impact the body in a negative way resulting in disease and decreased life expectancy. It is important to understand that while a person's lifestyle doesn't affect the genes they pass on to their child, their lifestyle choices can affect the gene's expression which is also passed on to the child with the genes during conception. Therefore, a parent's poor lifestyle choices today can negatively affect at least one successive generation and possibly many more. Alternatively, a parent's good lifestyle choices today can impact positively on successive generations.

The relationship between the epigenetic and genetic processes can be explained using an analogy. First, think of a television station as a *gene* (the hardware); the sound and picture that the television station transmits as the gene's *expression* (broadcast signal); the remote control, dials and switches on the television as the epigenetic processes that can *modify* the way the transmission appears on the television and is received; and finally that the *modified* transmission will *impact* the viewer and their experience. Then, if you're old enough to remember the days when television programming stopped after midnight, you'll know that after the normal programming signed off for the night, a 'test pattern' would appear on the screen. Most test patterns looked like a dartboard with a bull's eye in the middle, similar to the one pictured in figure 1.

As you know, a television's picture and sound are adjusted in response to the environment by using the television dials or a remote control. For example, if it is dinner time, the television may be turned off; if the room is dark, the brightness setting can be changed up or down; if the room is noisy the sound can be increased – are you getting the idea? – many aspects of the broadcast signal or expression can be

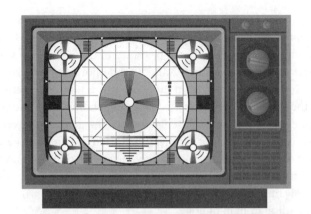

Fig. 1

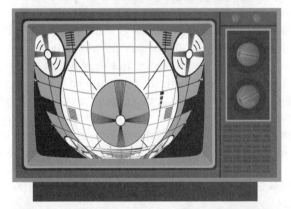

Fig. 2

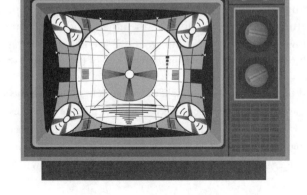

Fig. 3

adjusted based on the environmental influences and the viewer will get a different signal which will then have a different impact on them.

By adjusting the dials, the appearance of the pattern on the screen is altered as shown in figures 2 and 3 while not actually changing the original broadcast pattern from the gene. This is how epigenetics works. While the signals expression will change depending on the adjustments that are made to the settings (epigenetics), the gene as represented by the television station broadcast is unaffected … are you getting the picture?[1] Studies have shown that the epigenetic 'dials' can create over 30,000 variations of 'test pattern signals' from the same gene. This figure shows how important it is to consider epigenetic processes in relation to understanding human biology.

Poor lifestyle choices affect the gene's expression in the same way poor choices can be made to a variety of settings that affect the appearance of the television signal. Then, if a parent has adjusted the television setting based on their environment and then passes on this adjusted television set to the child, both the television and the current settings are received by the child. Some parents will pass on the television with settings which make for pleasant viewing and a positive impact on the child, others will pass on the television with settings which make poor viewing or worse still with setting that change the signal in ways that harm the child's eyes or ears. The child might even inherit a television which has been turned off where they get no signal at all. So what happens next?

If that child does not know how to change the settings and leaves the settings exactly the way they were received, it will then pass on the same settings to their offspring. On the other hand, if the child obtains new knowledge and understanding, and is then able to change the settings, they will pass on a different experience of the signal to their child.

---

1 To add further detail to this simplified explanation, in this epigenetic analogy, the test pattern on the television screen represents the protein backbone pattern encoded by a gene. While the television's controls can change the appearance of the pattern (figs 2 and 3), they do not change the original pattern of the broadcast (i.e. the gene). Epigenetic controls modify the readout of a gene without changing the DNA code.

It is important to remember, that the broadcast (gene) is unaffected by the changes in the television settings (epigenetic processes), so if they change the settings they can receive the original broadcast test pattern signal.

Now that you have an understanding of the process using the analogy of the television test pattern signal, we can relate this back to people.

Research that was carried out by a preventative-health specialist, Dr Lars Olov Bygren, found that parents' experiences, even early in their life could affect their children for generations to come. He studied the effects on children's eating patterns on their offspring. He found that children who experienced normal harvest years and then feast years, where they went from normal eating to 'gluttony' had sons and grandsons who lived shorter lives up to an astonishing difference of 32 years at the extreme. A shorter life was also found for the female children of gluttonous females. More recently, research by Pembrey, Bygren and Golding found that the sons of boys who smoked during puberty were at higher risk of health problems including obesity and a shorter lifespan. While it is hard to believe, what this research actually shows us is that a poor lifestyle choice of gluttony or smoking as a child can have a significant negative impact on future generations (Cloud 2010).

On a brighter note, it is important to remember that the opposite is also true. Those children who did not indulge in a gluttonous lifestyle and did not smoke during puberty, had children that were healthier and lived longer. Another example where a positive lifestyle change in the parent can influence the offspring positively is evident in an experiment that was carried out on mice. The scientists conducting the study used mice with a known genetic memory problem and put them in a supportive learning environment with toys, exercise and lots of attention. They found that these mice showed an improvement in something called long-term potentiation (LTP) which is a key factor in memory development. The important part was that their offspring showed this same improvement even though they received no extra stimulations using toys and exercise and attention. So what this means is that the developmental improvements the parent mouse made as a response to their supportive environment, was passed on to their offspring! While there was no change to the gene itself, there was a change to the gene expression and the positive change was passed on. This is epigenetics at work!

What does this all mean for parents who are preparing for conception? While it is frightening to know that poor lifestyle choices made as a child can affect future generations, it is also important to acknowledge that this is one of the most profound and empowering discoveries of our time. It is empowering as epigenetics transforms our old beliefs about genetics based on Darwinian theories.

Based on the concepts of Darwin's evolution of the species genetics go through an extremely slow evolutionary change over generations based on the survival of the fittest as they adapt to their environment. What this suggests is that people simply inherit genes and they are stuck with them. So if you inherit *good* genes you are healthy and if you inherit *bad* genes you are ill. This means that people are a victim of their genes – the genetics inherited control us. Darwinian beliefs mean that people are predisposed to ill health or good health based on the genes inherited.

However … the good news is that epigenetics changes all that! In a recent research study on men with prostate cancer risk (Ornish 2008), in only three months of lifestyle changes in diet, exercise and stress management, the participants in the study experienced changes in the activity of 500 genes. The activity of disease-preventing genes increased while a number of disease-promoting genes shut down, including those involved in prostate cancer and breast cancer.

These findings are inspiring and empowering as epigenetic processes show that we are actually the master and not the victim of our lives, given our genetic expression can be changed based on the way we respond to the environment and the lifestyle choices we make. The great news is that you no longer need to believe that any negative genetic expression you have inherited has to persist in your own life and so it follows then that it doesn't have to be passed on to your child!

Now if you are a parent hearing this information for the first time, you may be thinking that if you had known this information prior to becoming a parent, you could have done so much more to give your child a better start in life. This is true – as we know everyone is smarter in hindsight and can make more informed choices when they have more knowledge. However, it is also important to remember that epigenetics offers hope as it is empowering to know that nothing is permanent – you can help your child change their genetic expression by the way you help them to manage their responses to the environment. How to achieve this is discussed in many of the chapters in this book.

For those of you who are preparing for parenthood – you now know that you can give your child the best start in life by preparing your body to be the best it can be both physically and emotionally prior to conception. In this way you give your child the greatest chance to lead an inspired life – you help them start their life from a point of strength and not weakness. While no parent will ever be perfectly ready for parenthood – armed with this information, they can prepare in a sincere and mindful way rather than going headlong into parenthood ignorant of the possible negative effects poor lifestyle choices can have on their child's entire life and even their grandchildren's lives.

While the importance of preparing before conception is relatively new to science and modern cultures, it is not new in traditional cultures. People from these cultures have traditions and perform various rituals to prepare for conception and parenthood. For example, *The Tibetan art of parenting* (Brown et al. 2008) describes the Tibetan rituals and a purification process before conception which include preparing their bodies by eliminating toxins and eating nourishing foods, saying special prayers, attending to emotions, clearing the mind, connecting with spirit and inviting a child into the womb and family. They believe that these practices influence the nature and quality of the child who will be born to the couple.

To sum up the main points from this chapter, if you already have a child, the information in this chapter allows you to understand more about yourself and your child. The most important thing to remember is that even if you feel you have made poor lifestyle choices that have potentially impacted your child in a negative way, almost every gene expression is changeable. When you make positive lifestyle choices and support your child to make positive changes, the genetic expression for both you and your child can change. The changes can have a positive impact both physiologically, cognitively and emotionally. This is so empowering. You can see how this knowledge and understanding gives you choice and power to change your future and your child's the future for the better.

If you are preparing for parenthood then part of your preparation is to find a supportive parenting partner – one who will work with you to uncover subconscious negative programs and create more supportive programs. This will enable both parents to prepare themselves emotionally and physically for the conception of their child. As part of the preparation process, both parents need to be in the best physical and emotional states in order to give their child the best start in life. It is important to remember that poor lifestyle choices can affect the parents' genetic expression and this expression can be passed on to future generations with effects like increased chance of disease and shorter lifespan. Knowing this information is empowering for parents-to-be. It allows them to make informed choices when preparing for conception and parenthood which will enable them to give their child the best chance in life by giving them a strong foundation.

To conclude, as a parent-to-be, once you have found your parenting partner, prepared yourself to conceive your child, and have conceived your child (congratulations!), it is important to gain a good understanding of how the mother's experience during pregnancy can either positively or negatively impact on your unborn child at not only at birth but throughout the child's life. This is the subject of the next chapter.

Further readings

Brown AM, Farwell E & Nyerongsha D (2008). *The Tibetan art of parenting: from before conception through early childhood.* Boston: Wisdom Publications.

Cloud J (2010). Why your DNA isn't your destiny. *Time Magazine,* Wednesday, 6 January. Retrieved 4 August 2011 from www.time.com/time/magazine/article/0,9171,1952313,00.html.

Lipton BH (2005). *The biology of belief: unleashing the power of consciousness, matter and miracles.* Santa Rosa, CA: Mountain of Love/Elite Books.

Lipton BH & Bhaerman S (2010). *Spontaneous evolution: our positive future (and a way to get there from here).* Alexandria NSW: Hay House Inc.

Ornish, D (2008). Changing your lifestyle can change your genes. *Newsweek,* The Daily Beast, 17 June. Retrieved on 4 August 2011 from www.thedailybeast.com/newsweek/2008/06/16/changing-your-lifestyle-can-change-your-genes.html.

2

Managing stress during pregnancy

Dr Monique Robinson

It is every parent's wish for their child to be psychologically and emotionally healthy. For a large number of children, however, the statistics show otherwise. The World Health Organization (WHO) recently released figures suggesting that almost one in five children around the globe will experience some form of a behavioural or emotional problem during their childhood and adolescent years. Given a large number of children experience these problems, many parents, relatives, medical practitioners, friends or teachers will directly or indirectly come in contact with these children on a regular basis. Take a moment to think about how many children in your life show behavioural and emotional problems. Are you experiencing or have you experienced directly or indirectly the stress, the difficulties and the challenges these problems can cause for the children themselves and so many others in their life? As a researcher and a clinical psychologist working in the field of child and adolescent mental health I have experienced these at first hand.

In order to begin to address the issue of behavioural and emotional health problems in children, it is important that we understand how they develop. Over the years I have read and conducted many studies that contribute to our current knowledge. This chapter provides a summary of the key findings of this research (Robinson et al. 2011, 2008). It starts with a brief introduction and description of the common behavioural and emotional health problems in children before exploring how stress during pregnancy can affect the unborn child. For most people, stress is an ever increasing part of day-to-day life and pregnancy can result in even more stress, so most importantly, this chapter ends with suggestions on how mothers might reduce their stress levels and therefore reduce the possible negative effects on the child. By increasing our understanding through research, we can play an active role in reducing or preventing the existence of emotional and behavioural problems in our children.

Behavioural and emotional problems: an overview

Anxiety, depression, conduct disorder, attention deficit disorders and hyperactivity are common behavioural and emotional problems in children. The symptoms of childhood anxiety include being fearful, self-conscious, nervous, worried or feeling unlovable unless they are perfect. Anxiety can also lead to further difficulties. For example, if allowed to continue and escalate, over time it can lead to depression.

Depression is recognised by symptoms such as loneliness, crying, withdrawal from others, feeling unloved, guilty, sad or worthless and, in worst cases, it can even lead to a child taking their own life. It is frightening to know that in many western countries suicide rates for children are increasing. Other behavioural and emotional problems are also increasing, such as attention deficit disorder (ADD) and attention deficit hyperactivity disorder (ADHD), with symptoms such as difficulty concentrating, having trouble sitting still, poor school work, impulsiveness and daydreaming. Children with conduct disorders, which is a type of behavioural disorder, can be lying, missing school, running away, cheating, breaking rules, stealing, showing a lack of guilt and remorse, arguing, attacking others, distrusting others, and demonstrating general disobedience within the family and community.

Most people, especially parents and teachers, would argue that every child at one time or another, displays one or more of these behaviours but this does not mean they have an emotional or mental health problem. However when these behaviours occur regularly, are clustered together, and affect the child's functioning, this can often indicate a behavioural problem. The issue for pediatricians, child psychologists and families, is that although there is an increase in the number of diagnoses of these problems being made, and sometimes very early in childhood, we are still not certain why such problems and disorders develop. Research shows that mental, behavioural and emotional health problems occur across all social classes and all sorts of families so the stereotype that 'bad' families are responsible for a child's misbehaviour is just not true.

This chapter summarises a relatively new area of research that focuses on pregnancy, given it is one of the earliest influences on a child's development. The discussion centres on exploring the relationship between a mother experiencing stress during her pregnancy and her child developing behavioural and emotional problems. This research has the potential to explain the rise in these childhood problems we see all over the world today.

Stress during pregnancy: behavioural and emotional consequences for the child

You may not be aware that throughout history and across many cultures, the idea that a pregnant woman's emotions can influence the development of her unborn child is actually common. In contrast, the scientific evidence of emotions affecting the unborn child is only relatively new. This is because until recently, there was a scientific misconception, which is basically an incorrect belief, that the placenta which connects the child to the mother in the womb, provides a 'barrier' for the growing foetus that protects it from the mother's physical and emotional environment. Now that modern medicine has disproved this theory, huge advances have been made in our understanding of the short- and long-term negative consequences for the child if they are exposed to harmful conditions while in their mother's womb.

Summarised below are a number of studies which provide insights in the many aspects of the relationship between experiences during pregnancy and the negative effects on the behavioural and emotional development of the child. A variety of studies are explored which examine the effects of poor nutrition, different type of stress, the amount of stress and the timing of stress with interesting findings.

Poor nutrition

To some readers it may seem like science fiction that, how well we function later in life could be determined to some degree before we are even born. But a growing field of research, called the Developmental Origins of Health and Disease (DOHaD), has provided evidence to confirm that during pregnancy, the unborn child is not just a passive bystander, but is actually actively responding to changes within its environment in the mother's womb.

Through this research we are given amazing insights into how humans can adapt to their future environment, even before they are born. For example, when a mother does not receive enough nutrition during pregnancy, the unborn child is nutritionally deprived in the womb and is programmed for a life of poor nutrition in a world where there may not be enough to eat. In developing nations, such as India, where the food supply is not always plentiful, this is more likely. Yet in places like India, the shift from a life where food is in very short supply to a life where fast food and western-style food is increasingly available, has been very rapid. The DOHaD theory suggests that the child prepared in the womb for a 'life of thrift' is physically unprepared for a 'life of plenty' and this is why Asian nations are observing such frighteningly rapid increases in obesity, type 2 diabetes and mental illness. In this way we can see how conditions even before the child is born can affect the child for their entire life and that the programming is intended to improve the child's chance of survival in the world.

While medical researchers and public health professionals have been actively examining the influence of malnutrition in the uterus on a child's subsequent physical health for many years, only very recently has this research been considered relevant in mental health. Now the effects of influences on the unborn child are being studied in relation to their effect on the child's behavioural and emotional wellbeing. Some of the most important and insightful findings have come from research known as the Dutch Hunger Winter study (Susser et al. 1998), which provided the foundation for understanding how events that occur to the mother while she is pregnant can later affect the behavioural and emotional development of her child.

The Dutch Hunger Winter occurred between October 1944 and May 1945, when the German army stopped food supplies going into Holland in order to punish the Dutch people for assisting in the Allied forces' invasion of Europe. The major cities affected in western Holland included Amsterdam, Rotterdam, Utrecht and The Hague. Before and after the blockade, food supplies in the affected regions had been adequate, but during the months of the blockade, supplies became scarce and a number of women who were either pregnant or conceiving during this time would not have been able to eat enough food to have adequate nutrition. It is also not unreasonable to believe that this lack of food and the general environmental conditions were likely to be highly stressful for pregnant women.

Some time later, during the 1960s, all Dutch male children were called on their 18th birthday for compulsory military service. This included some male children who were born from pregnancies during the famine. At the military centres, all were required to complete numerous psychological tests and so there was a great deal of information on psychological health that could be used in research studies. Then the results of the psychological tests were linked with the young men's dates and regions of birth providing vital knowledge about the long-term effects of malnutrition in pregnancy on the psychiatric health of children.

Studies using this data showed that psychiatric illnesses were higher in the young men who were in the womb during the famine than the general population rates. These men were at a higher risk of disorders such as schizophrenia, depression and bipolar disorder, addiction disorders such as alcoholism and drug abuse, and antisocial personality disorder, which is associated with criminal activity and violent behaviour.

While these historical research studies are interesting and relevant to developing countries, you could argue that they may not be entirely relevant to women living in the western world at present. They are however relevant to the extent that we now know that conditions experienced in the womb by the unborn child, can have long-term psychological and emotional effects.

Stress: a part of daily life

So what is relevant to today's western world? With increasing work hours, a general sense of daily life speeding up, a dramatic increase in technology-driven information and productivity, increasing demands on our time, not to mention global financial crises, it makes perfect sense to explore the effects of stress as an important factor when researching the effects of pregnancy on the long-term psychological and emotional development of the child.

As most women who have experienced pregnancy can vouch for, stress during pregnancy is common and can relate to many different things. Stress can be experienced as anxiety, or neurotic personality characteristics and it can also refer to stressful life events and experiences that require some change or adjustment in the pregnant woman's life.

Apart from the fact that pregnancy and birth can often be experienced as stressful events in their own right, pregnancy also begins a number of changes in the life circumstances of the mother (and the family as a whole). Changes could include reduced work hours or even not working at all, preparing for a change in her relationship with her partner, helping children adjust to the arrival of a new baby sister or brother and the most common stress, the need to reassess and manage the family's financial situation. Research on stress in pregnancy has shown that debt, family illness, death, having a close association with a person with drug or alcohol problems and separation from a partner are, unsurprisingly, the most common stressful life events. If you have ever experienced any of these events, pregnant or not pregnant, you will know at first hand that they can all create huge emotional upheaval and stress!

In recent years, results from studies around the world have painted quite a disturbing picture as to the long-term effects of stress during pregnancy. It has become clear that a mother's experience of stress during pregnancy is associated with negative consequences for the child's development. The effect of stress on the unborn child can lead to an increased risk of the development of behavioural and emotional problems, such as childhood depression, anxiety and conduct disorders, in a similar way that toxic substances such as cigarettes, illicit drugs and large amounts of alcohol have a negative effect on the unborn child's development.

Studies have shown that when a woman is exposed to stress during pregnancy her child is at an increased risk for developing attention deficit hyperactivity disorder (ADHD) and the experience of psychotic symptoms in adolescence, which are the same effects found in studies on mothers exposed to cigarette smoking and drug use in pregnancy. Experiencing traumatic or stressful events during pregnancy has also been found to increase the likelihood of developing schizophrenia later in life, which is similar to the findings discussed earlier on malnutrition during pregnancy.

To explore the effects of stress further, researchers have examined women who have experienced a major trauma during pregnancy, including some of the world's worst natural and man-made disasters.

Stress as a result of natural and man-made disasters

We are all familiar with the events of September 11, 2001 when four commercial airliners in the US were hijacked by al-Qaeda terrorists and flown into the Twin Towers of the World Trade Center and the Pentagon US defense headquarters, resulting in the deaths of almost 3000 people. This event was a source of enormous psychological trauma for pregnant women in the surrounding Manhattan neighbourhoods. Post-traumatic stress symptoms in pregnant women during the World Trade Centre disaster, were related to more babies being born with a smaller head circumference at birth.

Given that head circumference is a good indicator of brain volume, this provided evidence of the effect of major trauma on the unborn child's brain development. Brain development affects both emotional and cognitive development in children later in life. Similarly, studies in Canada on the effects of a natural disaster – a major ice storm in Quebec – reported that children who were in the womb and experienced the trauma associated with the ice storm, had decreased intellectual abilities when compared with children who did not have the experience and these findings held true when the children were two years old and again at six years old.

While some pregnant women may experience natural and man-made disasters, the most common stressful events in pregnancy are not terrorist attacks and ice storms, but everyday factors like financial pressures and relationship problems. The question remains – could the stress we experience on the *everyday end of the scale* also affect the unborn child of a stressed mother?

Back in the late 1980s, a unique study was set up in Western Australia by a number of medical researchers including Professor John Newnham and Professor Fiona Stanley who originally wanted to examine the effect of multiple ultrasounds on later child development. As part of the study, the women who participated were asked general questions about their lifestyle, including details on stressful life events they had experienced during their pregnancy. While they found that multiple ultrasounds turned out to have no effect on child development, the information they collected on the stressful situations and events the pregnant women experienced provided invaluable insights into the negative effects of stress in pregnancy on child development. In these studies a variety of aspects in relation to stress during pregnancy were explored including the *number* of stressful events, the *types* of stressful event and the *timing* of the stressful event during pregnancy. The important thing to bear in mind is that these studies explored the stresses that are commonly experienced in society today.

Number of stressful events

The effect of more than one stressful event in pregnancy was examined to determine whether there was a relationship between the amount of stress and the increase in child behavioural problems as reported in previous studies. A wide variety of possible stressful experiences were included, from the death of a friend or family member, to relationship problems, moving house, problems with older children or the pregnancy, job loss and financial worries.

In the beginning, many other influences were considered along with stress, such as cigarette smoking, family income, breastfeeding and the age of the mother. However, even after all of these other influences were taken into account, the most consistent finding for increased mental health problems, like anxiety, depression and conduct disorder in young children came from stressful experiences during pregnancy. The amount of stress was important as each extra stressful event the unborn child experienced made the child approximately 1.3 times more at risk of developing a mental health problem by the age of five years.

Given these results were so strong, another study was conducted that followed the children through to the age of 14, when mental health problems are more likely to arise. Once again, it was found that with each extra stressful event that the mother experienced during her pregnancy, the child was more likely to develop a behavioural or emotional problem by the time they reached adolescence.

These results suggest that the more stress the mother, and hence the unborn child experiences, the worse the outcomes for the child in relation to their emotional and psychological development. When women experienced six or more stressful events during pregnancy, their children were over four times more likely to develop a mental health problem by the age of 14, than children who did not experience the stress during pregnancy.

This study did not provide information about what type of stressful experience was more likely to cause these effects, so the next step was to explore the types of stress experienced by the mother.

Types of stress

It is important to understand the nature of the stress as it can help us understand whether some stressful events, such as those that usually only occur once like the death of a relative, are better or worse for the unborn child than those stressful events that the mother wakes up to and lives every day, like money worries and relationship problems.

The research showed that the one-off experiences, like death of a relative or friend and job loss, had a very similar effect on the likelihood of the child developing mental health problems as those stressful events that were chronic and present every day, like money and relationship problems. It should be noted, however, classifying stressful situations as acute or chronic and the level of stress was not without its challenges and therefore the results need to be interpreted with this in mind.

Of course another explanation is that mothers who report a stressful pregnancy may be more anxious mothers. A seminal study has found that around 15% of child behavioural problems can be attributed to clinical anxiety disorders in the mothers. Children model their behaviour on their parental examples and anxiety-related behaviours can be learned. Anxiety is particularly common amongst women during their first pregnancy, where their lack of prior knowledge and experience can lead to increased worry. Given the links between anxiety and depression, it has been suggested that maternal experience of anxiety could also enhance the likelihood of the mother being exposed to postnatal depression, which has the potential to become a negative influence on later child behavioural and emotional development in its own right.

The research so far has focused on the relationship between the types and frequency of stress during pregnancy and subsequent behavioural and emotional problems in children, the study below examines whether the timing of the stressful event has any impact on the later developmental outcomes for the child.

Timing of stress

Researching the timing of the stress during pregnancy is important to determine if there is a greater or smaller risk for the unborn child when the stressful event occurs earlier in pregnancy as compared with later in pregnancy. Despite the fact that critical stages for foetal development, such as periods of rapid brain and other organ development take place early in pregnancy, the study showed that stressful experiences for the mother in the first four months of pregnancy compared with stressful experiences for the mother at around the eighth month of the pregnancy had a similar impact on the likelihood of the child developing behavioural and emotional problems later in life.

To summarise, the results of these studies show that it does not seem to matter *when* stressful events occur during pregnancy, or what *type* of events occur. What seems to matter is that at least one stressful event occurs, and if many stressful events occur, the potential negative outcomes for the child are worse as they have an increased risk of developing a behavioural or emotional problem.

As a researcher and a clinical psychologist, I am well aware of the shocking nature of these findings and the devastating effects they can have on the parents who come to my practice to get help for their children with behavioural and emotional problems. At this point it would be helpful to reflect on these findings.

A moment to reflect

Do you have a child with an emotional or behavioural disorder? As you reflect on your pregnancy do you recall experiencing one or more major stresses? If you answered yes to both of these questions you might be feeling sad, angry, concerned, guilty or some other negative emotion. If so, know that this is a perfectly normal reaction and I experience it regularly in my practice from the parents I see. It is a good sign to be vigilant to stress and to recognise when life is becoming overwhelming, but stress does happen in all our lives, and feeling guilty or anxious about whether this stress has harmed the baby is almost never helpful for mother or child. Almost all women will find that they experience some stressful times when they are pregnant, in fact in our study the average number of stressful events experienced was two – not zero and not one. And yet not all children have behavioural problems, so it is really important to understand that while a lot of stress will increase the risk of problems, it doesn't mean that every child born from a stress-fuelled pregnancy will automatically go on to have problems.

So what makes the difference between the stressful pregnancies that lead to behavioural problems in kids and those that don't? The most important thing from my perspective is to explain to parents that regardless of exposure to stress the unborn child experienced in the womb, once they are born, the right nurturing environment can provide the child with enormous potential to change their course of development. This is known as 'developmental plasticity', which means that the brain can adapt and change as the child grows with the right environment and they can overcome the behavioural and emotional problems. In the other chapters in this book, numerous practical insights are provided into how parents can support their children to develop strong self-esteem, resilience, emotional intelligence and manage their behaviours.

The discussion so far has focused on the emotional and behavioural effects of stress during pregnancy on children. The next section explores the physiological effects and concludes with the steps we can take to reduce stress during pregnancy.

Physiological effects of stress on the unborn child

Based on the research findings discussed so far, if we accept that stress during pregnancy can have a negative influence on the child's emotional development and behaviour even before it is born, how can we explain what is happening? There are a number of physical changes that stress induces. The fight-or-flight response is the body's automatic physical response to stress situations where the person's survival is threatened. It is stimulated by increases in the stress hormones adrenalin and cortisol. For example, in the prehistoric era, when early humans were out hunting and came face-to-face with a sabre-tooth tiger, they had a choice to either run to escape or prepare to fight. In fight-or-flight state, the heart beats faster in order to aid faster circulation of blood around the body, breathing quickens in order for the lungs to receive optimum oxygen, the mind becomes hyper-alert to the surrounding environment and concentration on any one feature of the environment is reduced in favour of this broader attentional need. This process serves to give the individual the best possible chance to survive in the presence of a threat.

While it is unlikely that you have been surprised by a sabre-tooth tiger while going about your daily business these days, the presence of a tiger-like threat (too much work, not enough money, demanding boss, cheating partner, death of a loved one) may be a regular occurrence, and so the physical changes induced in your body from the stresses remain. When stressed or anxious, many people report feeling like their heart is going to 'beat right out' of their chest. Similarly hyper-ventilation, filling the lungs with oxygen, is a common symptom of anxiety, and slow breathing remains one of the most consistently successful tools used by clinical psychologists for relieving anxiety. Many people who are experiencing periods of stress lay awake at night and are unable to sleep. Stress also limits concentration – have you felt distracted and unable to maintain your attention when under pressure? The mind and body become hyper-alert when under stress no matter what 'tiger' you are experiencing.

The same occurs during pregnancy, when the mother is stressed the hormones cortisol and adrenalin are automatically activated. Cortisol increases are seen naturally during pregnancy, but stress can further increase the circulating cortisol levels in the body. Cortisol, like other substances, can cross the placenta and from there it has the potential to influence the development of the unborn child's brain. It has been proposed that when the unborn child is exposed to higher levels of cortisol in the womb, it adapts by altering its developmental processes to prepare for a world which its mother perceives to be stressful and potentially hostile. In effect, it prepares itself for fight-or-flight response while in the womb. Then, once the child is born, this learned adaptation appears as behavioural problems.

If we compare the symptoms of stress and anxiety as noted in fight-or-flight behaviour, to the behavioural problems such as conduct disorder and attention deficit hyperactivity disorder (ADHD) there are similarities. Further, research has shown that more children with ADHD are born to mothers experiencing higher levels of stress during pregnancy.

Behavioural disorders share the characteristic of difficulty maintaining attention and concentration. So if an unborn child experiences its mother's many stresses while in the womb, it adapts and prepares itself for a world that may be stressful by developing hyper-vigilance to its surrounding environment. Other behaviours and emotions appropriate to the presence of a threat could include difficulty maintaining attention to any one focus, excess energy, crying, helplessness, fear, worrying and aggression. These are common symptoms of child behavioural problems along with depression, anxiety, conduct disorder, ADHD and social withdrawal.

However, not all environments that a child experiences once it is born will be threatening. What are the consequences for a child born prepared for threats existing in 'normal life'? For example, what happens for this child in the classroom? The very characteristics that were developed as a positive adaptation for survival in the womb become serious problems in the home, the classroom or within any environment that requires sustained concentration and attention. The physiological effects of stress during pregnancy may go some way to explaining the manifestation of increased behavioural problems in the children of stressed mothers.[1]

Knowing all of this ... where to from here?

Unfortunately, it is impossible to suggest that women completely avoid stress, in the way that we would suggest women avoid cigarettes, drugs or alcohol in pregnancy. Stress is part of life and pregnancy in particular is a time of change and adjustment. So what do we do about helping mothers reduce their stress?

Outlined below are suggested ways to manage prenatal stress that I have learned through my research as well as my professional and personal experience with pregnant women.

Internal versus external world

Events happen! Natural and man-made disasters, wars, financial stresses, job loss, illness and death, occur on a daily basis somewhere in the world. We will all be impacted by one or more of these events at some time in our lives and pregnancy doesn't protect us from these events. The important thing to remember is that while a person cannot control what happens outside of themselves, they have the ability to control over how they *respond* to the event. Stress is a response to an event. You know yourself, if a vase smashes that you really didn't like because it came from your evil step mother ... when it breaks ... you may even smile. On the other hand, if a vase smashes that came from your darling grandmother who passed away recently and it is the only

---

1 It is important to acknowledge that postnatal circumstances such as alcohol and drug use in families and neighbourhoods, domestic violence and child abuse can also contribute to the child's subsequent emotional and behavioural problems. However, this is beyond the scope of this chapter.

thing you have left from her ... you may choose to respond with sadness and stress, *or* say something like, 'hey, it is just a vase ... no one can take the great memories I have of my granny away from me'.

The purpose of this example was not to trivialise stress and stressful events, but to illustrate that we do have control over our responses *if we choose* to do so. The first part of managing stress is recognising the symptoms of stress. A general feeling of being overwhelmed is probably the best indicator of whether or not any external events are causing stress. Once pregnant women can recognise they are stressed, there are many techniques including focused deep breathing, spending time with caring friends and family, meditation, yoga, listening to relaxing music, taking time out and light exercise to help them manage stress. If you are pregnant or thinking of becoming pregnant you can investigate and practise what method will work for you. These techniques can be useful not just while pregnant but can be tools for a lifetime ... especially when you need to maintain calm at times when your toddler is driving you crazy!

If there are a number of events that occur in your life during pregnancy that hold the potential for stress, like moving house, re-evaluating finances, or ceasing employment, then seeking help and asking for support from others can also help to minimise the impact. Women who are feeling overwhelmed are best placed to ask for help through their antenatal care provider and use the social support provided by friends and family to help relieve the stress. It is important to remember, that if pregnant women make a special effort to keep their stress to a minimum for the short duration of the pregnancy it can make a lifetime of difference to their child and their family! Small efforts now ... great benefits later!

Share the knowledge and insights from research

Many people don't even think about the effects of stress on the unborn child and others may still believe that the child is 'protected' from stress in the womb. So, given research has clearly shown that stress during pregnancy can have long-term negative effects on a child, the more people become aware of these findings, the more pregnant women can take steps to reduce their stress and the more people in their life can support them to reduce stress. In this way, family, friends, colleagues, bosses and everyone in society can support pregnant mothers to reduce stress and make a positive difference in future children's lives and society as a whole.

Once more people become aware of the research findings as a community, there is something all of us can do to help relieve stress during pregnancy. Pregnancy is a time where complete strangers often feel it is appropriate to give advice to pregnant women, and many women are surprised by how forthcoming people in the street can be in terms of the pregnancy dos and don'ts. Perhaps as a society we need to suspend our personal opinions in favour of providing support for pregnant women. We also need to reflect on the adjustments that pregnancy entails before passing judgment and become more aware of the pressure that women may be under while pregnant.

Rest

One way to reduce stress is to take the opportunity to rest whenever you can and especially when you feel stressed or tired. This is easier if you make the rest about the baby. For example, a woman I knew worked quite long hours when she was pregnant. The way she managed her energy was to make time everyday to rest for her baby's wellbeing, by closing her office door during her breaks and relaxing or napping on a bean bag.

Enlist a 'gatekeeper'

After years of trying, one of my patients was very excited to learn that she was finally pregnant, right as she and her husband were in the midst of extensive renovations on their house. While for the most part my patient was able to handle the stress of living in a small part of the house while the renovations continued, she came up against a hurdle when a costly error was made in the building process and the contractors involved refused to take responsibility. The negotiations between parties began to cause enormous stress. The solution? We suggested that the patient enlist her husband as 'gatekeeper' and hand over all responsibility for sorting out the error to him. Although not solving the problem immediately, as it was going to take time to resolve, this strategy meant that my patient didn't need to be involved in the stressful negotiations and had some relief from the day-to-day hostilities. There are many more simple situations during pregnancy where a gatekeeper can help, such as saying 'no' for you when you feel overloaded with commitments, or delegating responsibility for projects or tasks that are causing stress. Remembering that there are others in your life who are willing to support you can reduce the likelihood of becoming overwhelmed.

Self-induced stress

Stress may come from women who are a little *too* concerned about making and raising the perfect child. That is, those who want to do everything right. In this way, the pregnant woman can be her own worst enemy and create her own stress! As already mentioned, pregnant women are inundated with information in medical and social contexts about the dos and don'ts of pregnancy. Abstaining from alcohol, quitting smoking, improving overall diet, avoiding certain foods, and increasing iron and folate, are some of the guidelines aimed at improving maternal lifestyle in pregnancy for the sake of the unborn child.

The dietary recommendations in particular have enormous potential for misinterpretation, whether it is the threat of Listeria lurking in soft cheese, avoiding salads and raw eggs or fish that have been soaking up mercury at the bottom of the ocean, such as salmon and tuna. It is important to keep a balance and follow guidance where possible but not take it to the extreme where it becomes obsessive and stressful. It has gone too far if you relate to stories of pregnant women seeing soft cheese on a platter at a party and leaving the party in fear that the soft cheese has contaminated all of the food or pregnant women waking up from nightmares featuring glasses of sauvignon blanc and having to reassure themselves that it was 'just a dream'. While all this stems from a desire to 'do the right thing' for the unborn child, the best thing is to keep a balanced perspective on things and manage rather than add to your stress.

Planning in advance

While it is difficult to know how much adjustment the pregnancy is going to involve, and how much stress those adjustments could potentially cause, some preparation and actions in advance might reduce the stress. For example, pregnancy usually entails the mother's temporary suspension of employment and this may bring with it a financial adjustment as the family moves from two incomes to one. For some women, this change can be facilitated easily without much resulting stress, or perhaps they have other children and have previously worked out a plan for subsequent pregnancies. For others the loss of one income can be catastrophic for the family finances. With some planning, part-time employment, working at home, family members helping out with free childcare can reduce the stressful thoughts of a difficult future during pregnancy. Unplanned pregnancies may be more likely to require planning and adjustments, such as moving to a more suitable house or support with respect to relationship pressures as the couple adjust to the unexpected impending arrival of their baby. In the first chapter of this book, Bruce Lipton talks about preconception and offers ideas to help prospective parents prepare for pregnancy and give their child the best genetic start in life.

Benefits to the whole of society

It is clear that there is increasing evidence as to the long-term negative implications of the mother's experience of stress during pregnancy which can alter the course of a child's emotional and behavioral outcomes. Pregnancy is a unique period of development and it presents a number of opportunities for intervention to support the mother, child and the family. Can early intervention support society as a whole?

The work of economist and Nobel Laureate James Heckman has detailed the benefits of early intervention in child development and Heckman recently co-wrote a study (Doyle et al. 2009) that extends this further by proposing the 'antenatal investment hypothesis'. This hypothesis proposes that not only would investing in interventions aimed at improving child developmental outcomes early in the child's life show significant advantages for the individual and society, but investing during the antenatal period shows greater economic gains than interventions after the child is born.

The many advantages from such investment include personal benefits, such as improved outcomes for cognitive development, behaviour and educational attainment, and also social and governmental betterments such as reduced crime and decreased social welfare spending. So basically, *we all benefit* by considering the developmental origins of health and disease and in particular, the effect of stress during pregnancy. Clearly, supporting pregnant women to understand the effects of stress exposure is vital: not to make them 'stressed about being stressed', but to support them in overcoming the pressures they face during this sensitive time and allocate resources towards this support in the community. In doing so we all play a role in helping stem the flow of child behavioural and emotional problems.

Further readings

Doyle O, Harmon CP, Heckman JJ & Tremblay RE (2009). Investing in early human development: timing and economic efficiency. *Economics & Human Biology*, 7(1): 1–6.

Robinson M, Mattes E, Oddy WH, Pennell CE, van Eekelen JAM, McLean NJ, Jacoby P, Li J, de Klerk NH, Zubrick SR, Stanley FJ & Newnham JP (2011). Prenatal stress events and behavioural development from age two to 14 years: The influence of the number, type and timing of stressful life experiences. *Development and Psychopathology*, 23(2): 507–20.

Robinson M, Oddy WH, Li J, Kendall GE, de Klerk NH, Silburn S, Zubrick SR, Newnham JP, Stanley FJ & Mattes E (2008). Pre- and postnatal influences on preschool mental health: a large-scale cohort study. *Journal of Child Psychology & Psychiatry*, 49(10): 1118–28.

Susser ES, Hoek HW & Brown A (1998). Neurodevelopmental disorders after prenatal famine: the story of the Dutch Famine Study. *American Journal of Epidemiology*, 147(3): 213–16.

3

Raising healthy and happy babies

Janette Roberts

It's every parent's wish to raise a healthy and happy baby. I've been blessed to raise two babies who are now wonderful young men. Over the years I've researched, personally experienced, written on the topic and shared the journey of raising babies with many families. In this chapter I'd like to introduce the main issues which I consider important for raising healthy and happy children. They include: the importance of community, following natural parenting instincts, preconception healthcare for prospective parents, minimising stress, prolonged breastfeeding, co-sleeping, keeping your baby close and creating a safe and nurturing home environment.[1] I believe that the more you understand about raising healthy and happy babies, the better choices you can make and the better chance you have of giving the adults of tomorrow the best start in life.

The role of community and parental instincts in raising babies

Until recently, the way in which babies were nurtured was universally similar, although that nurturing varied from culture to culture. Conception and pregnancy were integral and natural parts of life. Babies were born at home and lived with an extended family. They were carried close (and constantly) during their early months and were part of the ebb and flow of daily life. They slept in the family bed and

---

1 For further information please refer to the recommended reading list provided at the end of this chapter.

were breast-fed ad lib until weaning was initiated by them. This meant the responsibility, the knowledge and experience of raising babies was shared.

So you can imagine that in a community like this, mothering and fathering were simply part of everyday life and parenting was experienced and put into practice naturally and instinctively. In this environment you would learn from the close and constant contact with all the members of that family. You'd be intimately familiar with the continuum of pregnancy, birth, breastfeeding, weaning and nurturing, and by the time your first baby arrived, parenting would be second nature to you.

Today, babies spend less of their early years surrounded by the extended family members (including siblings, grandparents, uncles and aunts) and are likely to be more separate from the ebb and flow of family life. Many babies are raised less by communities and more in community day care. Furthermore, parents who have an intimate knowledge of and intuitive response to the continuum of child-raising before they have a child of their own are the exception rather than the rule.

So if you're wondering where your parental instincts have gone, it's not hard to see why. Having difficulty tuning into those responses is part of being a parent today. You now appreciate that many people have lost the experience of community support in raising a baby, that we live in an age of information and technological overload and finally, your preparation for conception (or otherwise), and your experience at birth and during breastfeeding also play a part in how well you're able to follow your natural instincts.

But an important step in raising babies is to trust those instincts, because your inner voice is wiser than you think! However, overabundance of information on every conceivable aspect of parenting can dampen your ability to hear that voice. Today, you're surrounded on all sides by a plethora of authorities offering parenting advice that is not only contradictory in many cases, but may also be in direct conflict with what is also called your 'gut' feeling.

Nevertheless, there are ways to cut through all the information and advice and tap into your instinctive response. For example, if the procedure you're offered, or the advice you're given, makes you feel uneasy, stop for a moment and ask yourself 'How do I really feel?' Silence your left, thinking, brain and listen to your inner voice. Put yourself mentally into each situation. One choice will probably give you an uncomfortable feeling of doubt and concern, and the other, an inner feeling of rightness. Do these simple exercises whenever you're confronted with a choice and the more frequently you do them, the more attuned you become to those instinctive responses that have guided parents for millennia.

Tuning out the left-brain, thinking response is good, but there's another fundamental factor to consider in relation to honing your natural instincts. Research has identified specific nutrients that have a profound bearing on the presence (or absence) of instinctive response. For example, an adequate supply of the trace elements manganese and zinc is necessary for formation of the hormones that underpin maternal instinct.

Maternal instinct also works best when your baby is born in robust good health, which is why preconception healthcare for both partners is such a vital part of your preparation for pregnancy. Sadly, increasing numbers of children suffer from subtle problems that can make instinctive mothering very difficult indeed. For example, a zinc-deficient baby (who cries excessively and is difficult to settle) will be unlikely to evoke an appropriate maternal response in his zinc-deficient mother (who may be suffering from postnatal depression).

Many parents believe that a diet that includes fresh fruit and vegetables will ensure good health for themselves and their unborn baby. Unfortunately, even a well-balanced diet may fail to support optimally healthy reproduction. Non-sustainable farming practices, refining and processing of food, alcohol and caffeine, the use of oral contraceptives and a stressful lifestyle are just some of the many factors that contribute to nutrient deficiencies (which includes deficiencies in zinc and manganese). Consequently, a well-balanced, comprehensive, multivitamin and mineral supplement that is specifically designed for reproduction, is required to ensure that you receive an adequate supply of all essential nutrients from before conception to breastfeeding and beyond. Consult with your natural-health practitioner and start on your supplementation well before you conceive. This supplementation, together with improved diet, healthy lifestyle and a non-toxic, stress-free environment will give you the best chance of a natural conception and support a healthy body for your unborn baby's early growth and development.

You have a better chance of raising happy and healthy babies when both of you take the time to prepare for the conception of your child and when you maintain that healthy status throughout your pregnancy and during breastfeeding. Consciously committing to and accepting responsibility for the health of your baby from his very earliest days also establishes firm foundations for trusting your instincts when that baby is finally in your arms. This is a great start to navigating parenthood, and to evaluating and embracing the information and advice in a way that is best for your family. When you heed that inner voice, parenting becomes a real joy, but that joy can be lost in times of stress. No parent or child likes feeling stressed but in a rushed and chaotic world, stress affects everybody – and especially babies.

Reduce stress: it's bad for everyone

As you read in the previous chapter, your unborn baby responds in profound and readily measurable ways to stress, so it's important to avoid or reduce stress levels before conception and particularly when you're pregnant. It makes sense that breastfed babies will also respond unfavourably when you're stressed! A stressed mother leads to a stressed baby, which in turn stresses the mother even more. This can stress the other parent and a cycle of family stress gathers momentum.

Stress actually comes in several forms – there are the physical and chemical stressors that come in the shape of environmental toxicity and unhealthy lifestyle habits. Electromagnetic radiation falls into this category, and so does lack of appropriate exercise. But stress of the mental and emotional variety is the type most usually associated with the word and even pleasant, much-anticipated life events such as a holiday or wedding can be stressful. For some mothers, natural activity like breastfeeding creates stress. Do you worry about how much milk your baby is getting, whether he's growing as quickly as a bottle-fed baby and how you'll manage his feeds when you go back to work?

But there's one certainty ... the more stressed you become, the less able you are to deal with stress. What's more, most of the things that you turn to in a stressful situation, such as cigarettes, coffee or sweet sugary snacks, are not only things you should be avoiding before you conceive and while you're pregnant or breastfeeding, but they will also exacerbate the problem. Then you can find yourself and the rest of the family in a downward spiral.

Stress has an adverse effect on nutrition via a number of pathways, with anti-oxidants and trace elements such as zinc particularly affected. Other victims of stress include vitamin B-complex, vitamins C and E, calcium, magnesium, potassium and sodium. Stress also affects eating patterns, at exactly the time when you need a really healthy, well-balanced diet. Nutritional losses and poor dietary habits mean that you're less able to deal effectively with the stress and so it goes on. One good way of dealing with stress is to ensure that your blood sugar levels are stable and that your nutritional status is adequate – that simply means some protein together with complex carbohydrates and some healthy oils at every meal together with that all-important nutritional support.

So what else can you do? Get familiar with some stress-reduction tools! Regular physical exercise is a great de-stressor. You might like to add a regular massage to your exercise routine, some acupressure or reflexology can be helpful, try tai chi or yoga or learn how to meditate. Today there are some great CDs that can get you to that positive meditative state very easily. Sitting quietly listening to classical music is another option (great during pregnancy for your baby in utero), but whatever you do, it needs to be something which is a regular part of your life.

Another great way to reduce those stress levels is to consciously take time out from everything in a relaxing environment when you feed your baby. Take this time to simply de-stress and be with your child. Put on some soft music, dim the lighting and breathe deeply. Try to focus only on your baby and take deep relaxing breaths which will help you quiet that busy mind and the constant stream of thoughts. Remember that the beneficial oxytocin that is flowing to both of you when you're breastfeeding is a powerful ally in switching off your left-brain function and allowing you to respond intuitively.

Oxytocin is also a powerful stress-reducing tool, it provides the direct antidote to the adrenaline fight-or-flight hormones that are produced when you're stressed. Oxytocin promotes calm, connection and intimacy with your baby and is just one of many good reasons for prolonging the breastfeeding period. Oxytocin is mothers' valium.

Sex is also a great de-stressor and that's oxytocin at work again – it's also the hormone produced at orgasm! However, sex can take a back seat for a while when there is a small baby or children in the house. Sex is also likely to be on the back burner while you're breastfeeding as mothers who breastfeed experience regular doses of oxytocin and may not experience a desire for sex.

I found that when I was breastfeeding I was awash in a sea of oxytocin so it was logical that I didn't feel the need for an extra dose, courtesy of my partner. He was a very understanding man – once he recognised the reasons. Another fundamental stress-reducing measure is sleep – but again this may be something that is in short supply when your children are young. The sleep equation I kept in balance with 'the family bed' and never missed an opportunity for a nap when my very busy and wakeful babies caught some shut-eye.

So regular sex, as much sleep as you can manage (naps work well), good eating habits, and regular exercise are all fundamental to reducing stress levels. Then you can add the special approaches that appeal to you! Even your partner or older children can give your neck and shoulders a massage (which will also promote oxytocin production).

Breastfeeding

Families make choices about breastfeeding or bottle-feeding their babies based on their knowledge and personal circumstances. The aim of this section is to outline the many benefits of breastfeeding, so that where there is a choice to be made, parents can make it from an informed position. It should also be emphasised that in speaking of breastmilk, the nutritional benefits are often highlighted while the more profound emotional, psychological and developmental benefits are given less airplay.

A recent study explored health professionals' knowledge of breastfeeding and the risks of formula feeding by looking at whether the findings in research studies were accurately conveyed in the titles and the abstracts of journal articles. The study was conducted by researchers at the Australian National University and found that of the 78 studies that reported *poorer health* among formula-fed infants, only 11% of the abstracts actually identified formula feeding as a health risk exposure. More shockingly, in 30% of cases, titles misleadingly implied that breastfeeding raised health risks. Given health professionals are busy it is plausible to assume that they may only have time to scan the title and the abstract and therefore be misinformed. The article concluded that, if widespread, this skew in communication of research findings may reduce the knowledge of and support for breastfeeding by health practitioners (Smith et al. 2009).

Breastfeeding confers multiple benefits on both babies and mothers beyond nutrition and stress reduction. In addition to the production of oxytocin, prolactin is produced by the pituitary gland. This is the hormone that controls lactation but it also has a calming, sedative effect. Breastfeeding women and their babies get an unlimited supply of both these important hormones. In other words breast milk is not only advantageous for babies it provides benefits for the mother which can support the whole family.

It's also advantageous for the community and the planet. Breast milk is produced naturally and without any harm to the environment. Breast milk is an extraordinarily complex substance, and the interactions and psychological development that accompany the act of breastfeeding are equally complex.

While there have been many new developments and innovations in developing formulae, despite the manufacturer's best attempts to 'reproduce' breast milk, formula is not able to provide the same nutritional support for babies as breast milk. In fact, as discussed above, there were 78 research studies that found *poorer health* among formula-fed infants than breast-fed infants and that health professionals may not know this information when making recommendations to their clients.

Nothing could be worse for new parents than the death of their new baby. Recent research has shown a link between breastfeeding and *lower* risk of death in the postneonatal period (between 28 days old and one year of age). The doctors concluded 'promoting breastfeeding has the potential to save or delay ≈ 720 postneonatal deaths in the United States each year' (Chen & Rogen 2004). Far more significant however is the number of deaths in the developing world that could be prevented were formula not promoted to this market.

So if you have a choice to breastfeed or formula-feed your baby, then know that there are not only nutritional and emotional benefits for breastfeeding as outlined above, but that there is a relationship between breastfed babies and a lower risk of postneonatal death and that longer breastfeeding is associated with health benefits.

Statistics show that about 70% of Australian women wean their baby by six months of age. This is often when solid foods are introduced to the baby's diet. However, there are many benefits to extended breastfeeding beyond six months. For example, atopic diseases like dermatitis, food allergy and asthma are serious health issues, and increasing numbers of children suffer with them. Research has shown that extended breastfeeding (more than six months) when compared with formula-feeding resulted in a lower incidence of these atopic diseases (Saarinen et al. 1979).

Breastfeeding protects and reduces the severity of gastrointestinal, urinary tract and respiratory infections. It has also been shown to support a child's developing immune system and that the benefits for immunity and protecting infants against illness extends well beyond weaning (Heinig 2001).

Extended breastfeeding not only offers health benefits but also supports a child's cognitive development. A recent study examined 17,046 healthy breastfeeding infants and 13,889 (81.5%) were followed up to six-and-a-half years of age. The study concluded '[t]hese results, based on the largest randomized sample ever conducted in the area of human lactation, provide strong evidence that prolonged and exclusive breastfeeding improves children's cognitive development' (Kramer et al. 2008, p578).

The evidence suggests that there are many benefits to continuing breastfeeding into toddlerhood. You may not be aware that the World Health Organization recommends breastfeeding for a minimum two-year period. So there's no rush to wean and I fed my boys for four-and-a-half and five-and-a-half years respectively, despite what the critics and doubters said – one day they simply walked away without any prompting from me.

However, if infant-led weaning isn't for you or your toddler, you can eliminate the feeds one at a time. Gradual weaning is easier on your baby's digestive system and avoids reactions such as tummy-ache which can result if he isn't given time to adapt to new foods. If you take your time weaning your baby, there are also fewer risks to you. Your breasts will naturally produce less milk as your baby suckles less. If you stop suddenly, this can cause your breasts to become engorged, which can be very uncomfortable.

One reason that mothers decide to stop feeding is because breast-fed babies are often small in comparison to a bottle-fed baby of the same age, and also smaller than a baby who's had solids from an early age. However, your smaller, fully breast-fed baby is not necessarily lighter than his bottle-fed counterparts. His bones are denser and he has a higher proportion of lean muscle, which means he's heavier. Remember too that fat cells are laid down in infancy and large, chubby babies may be in for a lifelong battle with excess weight.

Nevertheless, if you decide to wean your baby, it is recommended to avoid cow's milk which is the most common allergen. Moreover calcium, iron and other nutrients are actually poorly absorbed from cow's milk. Did you know that humans are the only creatures on earth that regularly drink the milk designed for another species?

Two thirds of the world's population cannot tolerate dairy foods and they get their calcium requirements from other sources. These include cultured yoghurt (which is tolerated better than milk or cheese by most people as it is pre-digested by the bacteria in the culture), tahini paste, green leafy vegetables and fish such as salmon and sardines (with the bones). Remember too that other minerals such as magnesium and zinc are important for the development of strong bones and teeth. Cow's milk will reduce your child's appetite for more nourishing foods. Goat's milk is a possible alternative if you choose to give your child a milk drink but soy is not a good alternative for reasons which have recently become apparent.

There has been a huge increase in the consumption of soy milk over the last 20 years, however we are now seeing an increase in the number of children who are allergic to it. Soy can also interfere with the formation of hormone receptor sites and should not be given to young babies (some authorities recommend no soy before 24 months). The high circulating concentrations of isoflavones (13,000–22,000 times higher than natural plasma oestrogen) may exert hormonal effects. The long-term effects in infants are unknown.

Now, if you're wondering what on earth you're going to give your child to drink, rest assured that purified water, as a thirst quencher, is still impossible to beat. When my boys were young I made cooled weak herbal teas and fruit smoothies with an over-ripe banana, some unsweetened yoghurt and water to give them a change from filtered water. You can always vary the flavour of smoothies by using a different variety of fruit, but stay away from or limit commercial fruit juices! In large quantities, fruit juices contain the sugar of tens of apples, oranges or pears and their consumption has been linked to dental decay, chronic non-specific diarrhoea (especially if sorbitol or other artificial sweeteners are present), stunted growth and obesity.

Now let's get onto the topic of solids! Is your baby ready for solid food? There are absolutely no benefits in giving your baby solids before six months of age. In fact, until he can sit up, he will find it difficult to digest them, as gravity has a part to play. The age at which he starts on solid food isn't a measure of his intelligence or any other developmental milestone and it's a myth that giving solids will encourage him to sleep through the night. In fact, several health problems can result if you start him on solids too early.

Your baby's digestive system matures slowly and many of the enzymes required for digestion are totally absent for many months.

Before six months of age your baby's gut is still permeable and foreign proteins that are a result of incomplete digestion of food can be absorbed through the intestinal mucosa. These foreign proteins then go on to cause allergies and intolerances to that food.

After about six months (but the time will vary quite a bit and it may be closer to eight or nine months) your baby makes his own secretory immunoglobulin A (IgA) which coats the intestines and stops the absorption of foreign proteins. Therefore the recommendations of experts (including the American Academy of Pediatrics [2005], UNICEF, WHO and others) is for exclusive breastfeeding for the first six months of life. However, experts working in the field of clinical ecology, recommend that you wait until 12 months before you introduce any of the major allergens to your baby's diet like eggs, cow's milk products, wheat, citrus fruits, strawberries or the nightshade family – potatoes, tomatoes, capsicums and eggplants especially if there's any history of allergy in either of your families.

I waited until my boys were reaching for food from my plate, which was about eight–nine months in both cases, then let them graze on healthy food (avoiding dairy, wheat, eggs and citrus for 12 months) rather than insist on three fixed meals a day. Breastfeeding continued to be their major source of nutrition for a long time. I kept my own nutritional status topped up with robust supplementation.

Sleeping arrangements

Now that your baby has been fed, let's move on to the very important topic of sleeping and I want to start with a poem that I wrote recently for a young woman's baby shower. The invitation to the party had requested contributions towards a cot for her soon-to-be-born

> You say a cot ...
>
> but maybe not?
>
> The family bed
>
> is good instead!
>
> For night-time feeds

and night-time needs.

Stay horizontal, warm & snug –

the nursery option is a dud!

Mum least disturbed,

Bub least distressed.

Don't leave your bed –

just bare the breast.

A side-car so she will not fall

or mattresses placed wall to wall.

It's easy, best ... what more to say?

Ignore the doubters who say nay!

The world has always slept this way ...

and she WILL leave your bed one day!

AND long before she goes to University – that's a promise :)

Co-sleeping option

'The family bed' or 'co-sleeping' is not a radical or trendy parenting alternative. It is simply sleeping in the same way that the human species has done for more than 99.99% of its time on this planet. For countless centuries, for countless families in countless countries, the family bed was simply the only way of sleeping. In other words, solitary sleeping arrangements for infants (and for adults as well) have been around for about as long as the blink of an eye in evolutionary terms.

Of course advances in technology and the changes in lifestyle which have occurred in the last 200 years have been so momentous and have propelled us all forward so quickly, that it is easy to forget that our biology hasn't kept pace. Many families work long and hard to afford separate sleeping quarters for all family members, and also consider this achievement an improvement in their standard of living. Those who are able to afford such 'luxury' are therefore likely to assume that the separation of adults from their children is without real consequence, or that the effects can only be positive.

But perhaps we should pay a little more attention to what we are really doing when we force children to sleep alone. James McKenna, Professor of Biological Anthropology and Director of the Mother-Baby Behavioural Sleep Laboratory, at the University of Notre Dame, US, says 'Solitary sleeping arrangements represent one of the least recognised, but certainly one of the most potentially significant cultural experiments of the 19th and 20th centuries, the consequences of which have never been scientifically explored' (McKenna & McDade 2005).

While co-sleeping has many benefits for the whole family, the nursing mother–baby dyad is actually biologically designed to sleep as a unit. James McKenna says that breastfeeding and co-sleeping are part of the same adaptive system that maximises infant survival and parental reproductive success. It is also beneficial for helping the parents get as much rest as possible, given it is natural for a baby to wake regularly through the night.

The brain of your newborn baby is still immature. In the early months of his life he will experience long periods of sleep from which he can be easily aroused. This means he will wake fairly frequently. This sleep pattern, which is unique to infants, is thought to be important for their brain development. Since that development continues rapidly until about three years of age when the brain approaches 90% of its adult capacity, it is unlikely that a healthy baby will sleep for an unbroken six or eight hours during the night.

It is also an unrealistic expectation that you will, without complaint, rouse yourself from deep sleep, rise from your warm bed and attend to your baby whenever he wakes. By giving your baby separate sleeping quarters, night-time becomes unnecessarily stressful and your baby is denied the things that he needs most – your warmth, the sound of your heartbeat, your touch and your breast.

Furthermore, a nursing mother and her co-sleeping infant have synchronised sleep and arousal patterns. This arousal-sleep-arousal cycle, which lasts about 90 minutes in an adult, is also the usual length of time between feeds for the co-sleeping baby. As a nursing mother and her child enter the light phase of sleep together, the baby will stir and start to suckle. He won't cry, since the nipple is within reach of his mouth and his mother's sleep is only slightly disturbed as she becomes dimly aware of him nursing. Then both return to a state of deeper sleep. With co-sleeping, crying is reduced in frequency and any crying periods are of shorter duration, nursing is well established earlier and the baby gains weight faster.

A co-sleeping baby also responds to his mother's breathing (or his father's) and his apnoea rate is reduced. All the mechanisms regulating respiratory rate, heart rate, oxygen saturation and other significant factors operate better when the baby is in direct contact with his mother. It seems then that co-sleeping is a tried and true parenting practice with real benefits for modern families, and is undoubtedly the simplest solution to attending to the very normal baby who continues to wake for feeds during the night.

My boys slept in our king-size family bed from the moment they were born. Both nursed through the night til they were about three years old and continued to sleep on our wall-to-wall mattresses for a while longer. My sleep was disturbed, but minimally, they were never reluctant to go to bed (being nursed to sleep), never had night-time fears or phobias and just as they walked away from the breast, they also walked away from the family bed – when they were ready. I attribute a great deal of the confidence and security that they have exhibited throughout their lives to these simple, stress-free, traditional parenting practices!

Co-sleeping precautions

While co-sleeping offers the many benefits as outlined above, research studies have shown that the risk of death is higher if the parent(s) smoke, consume alcohol or are heavy sleepers, and in these cases should not share a bed with their infant. Furthermore, other precautions include: no sofas, no waterbeds, no infant pillow, no use of heavy bedding or duvets or use of beds where the child could wedge its head between the bedhead or sides on the bed.

There are a number of studies that have reported that bed sharing increases the risk of sudden infant death syndrome (SIDS). A review of these studies by two medical doctors in 2004 showed that these studies did not take into account the other factors that are related to increased SIDS listed above. For example, risk factors include parental impairment (smoking or drinking) at the time of the infant's death, the infant's sleep position (face down), and whether the infant slept on an inappropriate surface such as a water bed or couch. They note that the few studies that have controlled for maternal tobacco and alcohol use have found little or no independent relationship between bed sharing and SIDS.

More importantly these same doctors argued that

> [a]lthough data supporting important adverse effects directly related to bed sharing are lacking, substantial data exist that bed sharing confers benefits to the infant, including improved breastfeeding, less infant crying, improved parent and child sleep, and improved parent-child bonding. Some of these factors, in turn, may relate directly to decreased risk of child abuse, one of the greatest health issues in pediatrics. (Gesner & Porter 2006)

It seems then, that under the right conditions, co-sleeping poses little or no risk for the infant but can provide many benefits for both parents and infants. However, if co-sleeping in the same bed is not the right choice for your family, then sleeping the baby in his own bed in the same room is a better option than sleeping in a room on his own. Research shows that room sharing with a committed caregiver reduces SIDS among SIDS-prone infants (McKenna & McDade 2005).

Keep your baby close and stimulate all your baby's senses: movement, sight, sound, smell, touch

As your baby grows he spends less time sleeping and more time awake. Then both parents will have more time to connect and engage with him, and support his development. Everything that your baby sees, smells, hears, touches and tastes is new and fascinating, and stimulates his neurological development. An infant learns by having all of his senses stimulated, so the more stimulation he receives the more he learns. It's important that your baby gets the widest possible exposure to all of these sensations so that he will fully comprehend and, later, manage his environment.

Carrying your baby as an extension of your body is the simplest way to make sure this happens. In this way your baby is an integral part of the family day and it's also the easiest way for you to get on with your life. I carried my babies (first front and then on my back) until they were too heavy to do it any longer! When your baby is tiny, a snuggly wrap that supports an upright posture with full leg support is what you need.

When he's snuggled close to your breast or perched over your shoulder it's impossible to ignore him and when you talk to him and let him be a part of all your activities during his early months, he is automatically subjected to a constant stream of sensorial stimulation. But in modern western society many babies receive reduced amounts of this sensorial input. If you put your baby down in a cot he can see nothing more than the coloured mobile swinging above his head. Lying in his pram he experiences only its monotonous movement and an uninterrupted view of a plastic canopy. Tucked away in his nursery, he can hear none of your conversations.

Separating your baby from the ebb and flow of life in this way denies him the opportunity to experience the complete range of sound, sight and movement. By confining him to a cot, a playpen, a pram or a push-chair, you bypass the opportunity to stimulate his touch, position and balance receptors. Nor are any of these situations conducive to the initiation of verbal or non-verbal dialogues that stimulate his cognitive processes, so by limiting his exposure to sensorial stimulation his learning and co-ordination are compromised.

Your baby will be more content when he can feel like he did when he was in your womb. This is good reason to pick him up and hold him. Studies confirm what is fairly obvious – babies cry less if they are carried more. This is not only much healthier for your baby's emotional and mental development, but at a much more practical level, it leaves both your hands free for other tasks.

Attend to your baby's cries and he'll feel safe

Crying is your baby's only means of communicating with you. When he signals, by crying, that he needs something and you immediately pick him up, you're telling him that you care about him and about his feelings. You're also letting him know that he is not completely powerless.

A crying baby stirs something deep and uncomfortable in me, even today when I hear a baby cry I get tense and want to do something to soothe it. Some people might say that by picking him up when he cries, you are spoiling him, but another way to look at it is that you are simply responding to his needs. You might also have noticed that leaving his cries unanswered actually goes against your instinct as parents. It doesn't feel comfortable to simply let a baby cry – it is a parent's instinct to respond and soothe. In responding, you're laying the groundwork for trust, respect and completely open lines of communication for all of your parenting years.

Create a nurturing home environment

Creating a harmonious and nurturing environment for your child to live in is another key aspect of parenting healthy and happy babies. When your child is ready for his own sleeping space, put yourself in his place and think how he'll feel before he falls asleep and when he wakes up – try to create a sense of safety and familiarity. The colours for his bedroom should be calming shades with pink, green or lilac being appropriate choices.

Full-spectrum lighting (as in daylight) is used as an essential nutrient by the endocrine system. So use daylight as much as possible for all your children's activities and incandescent lights where necessary, avoiding fluorescent lights where possible.

Try to keep your child's (and your own) environment in order, and reduce muddle and mess where you can. Take a leaf from Maria Montessori's book and give all his toys, games and activities a special place on easily accessible shelving in his room. A child quickly learns to replace an item from its designated spot (at least that's the theory and it certainly works well in the classroom) and actually takes great pride in doing so. Wherever possible, surround your child with cleanliness, order and beauty.[2]

---

2 For more information on the Montessori method of education refer to the

Introduce harmony through music and song. After your baby is born he needs exposure to the world, in all its variety and wonder, to stimulate his brain's development. Playing music and singing songs is a simple way to increase the amount of stimulation he receives. Music and song also have the ability to soothe, calm, improve mood, increase intelligence and develop memory. There are even studies linking the playing of Mozart to improvements in some brain functions. While there remains debate about how significant or long-lasting these effects might be, Shinichi Suzuki's widely recognised and applauded work through his Talent Education Research Institute has shown that musical ability is not inborn and that talent can be created (International Suzuki Association n.d.; see also Rauscher et al. 1995).

Having absolutely zip musical ability myself, my boys benefited from the classical music that I preferred to listen to from the time they were in utero. I had also decided (one of those intuitive 'hits' that I got when reading about the Suzuki method) that they would learn the violin. So from age three, music was a serious family commitment and despite moments of frustration both are now accomplished and passionate musicians. However, their preferred genre is heavy metal and their band The Eradicated undoubtedly a rebellion against all their years in classical training. They do however invite me to their gigs!

Foster exploration, independence and self-esteem

As your baby becomes more mobile, to foster exploration and independence you can modify his environment in a way that encourages him to explore this new, safe and interesting place. Let him feel that he has mastery over his environment by doing nothing for him that he can do for himself and he will soon master a number of skills and gain self-confidence with his increasing ability. Start by allowing him to do what he has watched you do from his earliest days. This will mean turning the pages on books and as his ability and curiosity grows, to open cupboards, take out plates and cups, turn on the television, adjust

---

Association Montessori Internationale website: www.montessori-ami.org or a Montessori association or school in your country.

the volume, put clothes in the washing machine, dust, sweep, and walk up and down stairs unaided. Whenever it is humanly possible, allow him to do these things and before you know it he'll be 16 and he'll want to drive the car!

Allow his explorations to lead him into the yard or to where there is mud, dirt and water. These expeditions will be enormously interesting and satisfying for him but he will have no regard for the fact that he will get impossibly dirty or that he might ruin his best clothes. You'll be wise to have as little regard for the mess as your child and simply remember that skin is very durable and easily cleaned.

The basis of your child's self-esteem is established in infancy. It begins with the body language that you display. The way in which you hold him, your facial expressions and tone of voice signal that he is loved and valued. When your baby has his cries answered he also knows that you care for him and feels that he is a worthwhile person. When you enable him to manipulate his immediate environment by doing meaningful things for himself, those positive feelings are constantly reinforced.

All of these positive feelings – love, security and emotional attachment – from you and a high degree of mastery over his environment go a long way to establishing your child's self-esteem. While it is not impossible to build self-esteem later in life, it is infinitely harder and if the groundwork is firmly laid in infancy and early childhood, then it is almost impossible to undo. It is far easier in those early years to make sure that your child feels really good about himself, than it is to try, during adolescence or later, to reverse a poor self-image.

If your child has high self-esteem then he has something very special – a strong sense of his own value which will support him to live as a fully functioning and well-adjusted member of society. The child that receives the gift of self-esteem in his or her early years will truly reap the rewards for all his days, and the wider community will benefit too! There is a chapter on self-esteem later in this book.

In so many aspects of my sons' lives I see the truth of this and the value of establishing self-esteem when children are young. In all my years of working and talking with other professionals, one thing stands above the rest. Establishing self-esteem in children happens naturally and easily when parents are confident to revert to some of the tried and true parenting practices that I've outlined here. Nature has designed an almost perfect system and we've tinkered with it to our own and our children's detriment.

A child with high self-esteem is less likely to bend to peer pressure and less likely to embrace the 'chemically enhanced' life to feel good about himself. Just as important, having high self-esteem means that he is more likely to choose what is right for him, rather than try to impress or placate others. When your parenting choices have given your child high self-esteem, you can be confident in the way he will conduct himself and in the choices he will make. Finally, feeling good about himself means he can reach out to nurture and support others and best of all he will always be nice to his Mum and Dad!

Further readings

American Academy of Pediatrics (2005). Policy statement: breastfeeding and the use of human milk. *Pediatrics*, 115 (2): 496–506.

Chen A & Rogen W (2004). Breastfeeding and the risk of postneonatal death in the United States. *Pediatrics*,113(5): 435–39.

Gesner B & Porter T (2006). Bed sharing with unimpaired parents is not an important risk for sudden infant death syndrome. *Pediatrics,* 117 (3): 990–91.

Heinig J (2001). Host defense benefits of breastfeeding for the infant: effect of breastfeeding duration and exclusivity. *Pediatric Clinics of North America,* 48(1): 105–23.

International Suzuki Association (n.d.). Retrieved on 31 August 2011 from internationalsuzuki.org/shinichisuzuki.htm.

Kramer M, Aboud F, Mironova E, Vanilovich I, Platt R, et al. (2008). Breastfeeding and child cognitive development: new evidence from a large randomized trial. *Arch Gen Psychiatry,* 65(5): 578–84.

McKenna J & McDade T (2005). Why babies should never sleep alone: a review of the co-sleeping controversy in relation to SIDS, bed-sharing and breastfeeding. *Paediatric Respiratory Reviews,* 6: 134–52.

Naish F & Roberts J (2002). *The natural way to better breastfeeding.* Milsons Point, NSW: Doubleday.

Naish F & Roberts J (2000). *The natural way to better birth and bonding.* Sydney: Doubleday.

Naish F & Roberts J (1999). *The natural way to a better pregnancy.* Sydney: Doubleday.

Naish F & Roberts J (1996). *The natural way to better babies: preconception healthcare for prospective parents.* Sydney: Random House.

Rauscher F, Shaw G & Ky K. (1995). Listening to Mozart enhances spatial-temporal reasoning: towards a neurophysiological basis. *Neuroscience Letters,* 185(1): 44–47.

Roberts J (2012). *Healthy parents, healthy babies.* Sydney: Random House.

Saarinen U, Backman A, Kajosaari M & Siimes M (1979). Prolonged breastfeeding as prophylaxis for atopic disease. *The Lancet,* 314 (8135): 163–66.

Smith J, Dunstone M & Elliott-Rudder M (2009). Health professional knowledge of breastfeeding: are the health risks of infant formula feeding accurately conveyed by the titles and abstracts of journal articles? *Journal of Human Lactation,* 25(3): 350–58.

UNICEF (n.d.). Infant and young child feeding. Retrieved on 31 August 2011 from www.unicef.org/nutrition/index_breastfeeding.html.

World Health Organization (n.d.). Exclusive breastfeeding. Retrieved on 31 August 2011 from www.who.int/nutrition/topics/exclusive_breastfeeding/en/.

4

Preparing children for life

Dr Rosina McAlpine

As parents, one of our main roles is to prepare our children for life. Sooner than we think, they leave our loving care to make their own way in the world. So, how do we prepare them for life? If you take a moment to reflect, perhaps you'll agree that your personal qualities and life skills play a key role in supporting you to live a successful and happy life. For example, your ability to learn, maintain a positive attitude, manage your behaviour, communicate with people, develop good relationships, set and achieve goals, take care of your health and bounce back after adversity are just some of the many life skills and personal qualities that have helped you succeed in your life. Given life skills and personal qualities are key for our children's success, it is important to explore where and when our children are developing these essential skills.

Today, a research-based approach to life skills development has been advocated for university education. Teaching approaches, based on sound research findings, enable students to develop skills and attributes in a whole range of areas including: continuous learning through researching, analysing and communicating knowledge, environmental awareness, self-evaluation and management, as well as the development of social skills such as being able to work inclusively with people from different cultures (Barrie 2004). While this is great news for our university graduates, not all children go to university, and those who do need to develop life skills well before they start their studies.

I've been a university lecturer for over 20 years and I can't tell you how many times I've heard my first-year students say things like the hardest thing about going to uni is not the work, it's that I've left home and:

- Mum used to do everything for me and now I have to do it myself!
- I don't know how to cook. I'm sick of living off two-minute noodles and takeaway.
- I've given myself salmonella poisoning by putting raw chicken on my salad board.
- I've ruined my clothes in the wash and all my white T-shirts are now pink!
- I feel really lonely and depressed.
- It's all too much I can't manage everything.
- I've just failed my exam and I've never failed anything in my life. I can't cope.
- I'm having trouble getting on with some people. I can't tell them how I really feel.
- I could always rely on my parents to pay for everything. Now, I can't manage my money so I'm broke.

And the list goes on.

When I was a girl, while my mum certainly did most of the work around our home, I still learned to cook and helped with the cleaning and the laundry. I knew that I had to separate the whites from the blacks and I knew to be especially careful of washing red clothes with anything white! If I wanted to buy something special like a new handbag, I had to work for it. I'd start with how much I needed, then work out how I could earn the money and I'd save until I reached my goal. I grew up in a family of six (parents and four children) and so we all had plenty of opportunities to learn about managing, delegating, sharing, conflict resolution and the art of negotiation.

As a parent I am very aware of how important it is for our son to develop key life skills so he is equipped to create a fulfilling and successful life for himself. I was also very curious to understand why so many of the young men and women I came into contact with at university simply didn't have essential life skills or the basic personal qualities that provide a solid foundation for life success. As a researcher and a life coach, I had access to many parents and began asking questions. My enquiry revealed that alongside the unique responses, there were also common themes which could explain why children weren't developing important life skills while growing up. The main themes are revealed in the comments below:

- When I was a child, I had to do a lot of chores and so I didn't feel like I had a childhood. That's why I decided early on to let my child be a child and play.
- From the time my children were very young, I had to work in order to make ends meet. Between work, getting the kids ready for school and taxied to their other activities, taking care of all of the things at home, I had so little quality time with the kids to help them learn life skills.
- Nowadays there is so much pressure on our kids to do well academically to get anywhere in life, they just don't have the time to help around the house.
- My children were so busy with school and sports I hardly spent time with them except when I was driving them from one activity to the next.
- I never really thought about whether my kids were developing life skills, I believed they developed them at school.
- I thought it was more important that my children had tutoring for subjects they needed help with, so that meant no time after school.
- Teenagers of today are in their own world, they don't seem part of the family they just want to listen to music, play video games, text on the phone and basically do their own thing.
- If my teenagers say they don't want to do something, what can I really do? In my day, I got a damn good hiding if I didn't listen and so I just did as I was told. Have you ever tried to negotiate with today's teenagers?
- I found it took too much time to show my kids how to do things around the house and I just didn't have the time. It was so much quicker and easier if I did it myself, and so I did.

If you have children, do any of these themes ring true for you? And like so many other parents, are you concerned about your children when you know that an increasing number of children are experiencing depression, bullying, obesity, suicide, behavioural problems such as attention deficit hyperactivity disorder (ADHD), and drug and alcohol abuse? Research provides some hope in that it shows that life skills education can reduce the risk of tobacco and substance abuse in school children (Botvin et al. 2003).

For most parents it's clear that their children need to develop key life skills and personal qualities in order to survive and to thrive in life from an early age. What may not be clear is determining which life skills children really need and how to help them develop these skills. This chapter aims to develop a new model based on a holistic approach to life skills education. This provides a foundation from which to build a comprehensive program for children's life skills education.

Key life skills and personal qualities

Research on life skills education tends to focus on developing skills in children with disabilities and special needs. There seems to be a hole in the literature when it comes to a systematic and holistic life skills education for children without special needs from preschool and throughout their education. Based on my research into child development, decades of experience in teaching university students, insights from coaching parents and children for over five years as well as my own experience as a mother, I have identified the following seven key areas for life skill and personal attribute development:

1. personal power: self-esteem and resilience
2. health and wellbeing
3. education, career and money
4. social and environmental understanding
5. communication skills and relationships
6. relaxation and play
7. inspired creativity.

Provided below is a brief explanation of the life skills in each of these categories. I have also included examples of activities you can try with your children to help them develop these key life skills.

1. Personal power

Personal power is about self-esteem and resilience, and relates to how children 'feel' about themselves and what they 'believe' about themselves. Children who don't feel sure of themselves or feel unsafe tend to shy away from new experiences. Children who don't feel good about themselves generally succumb to peer pressure, are bullied, behave defensively and feel insecure which often results in all kinds of negative behaviour, especially under difficult circumstances.

In contrast, children who feel good about who they are and believe in themselves, are more likely to try new things and bounce back after difficult experiences. Children who accept themselves are less likely to want to be like others and are more likely to discover what they can contribute. Our son is four so it's very important to me to help him develop his personal power early in life so he can continue to explore the world, learn from his experiences and develop as a person. Self-esteem, resilience and optimism can be learned and developed (Seligman 1997).

It is natural for children to look to their parents to learn about themselves and to discover how to act in the world. So parents are in a great position to help their children develop personal power. There are many simple ways to support your child's self-esteem including spending time with them and interacting in a caring way. These simple things show your child that you believe they are important and loved. They can then internalise your beliefs and behaviours, and love themselves. That is, if you believe they are important and lovable they must be important and lovable – because parents are always right. Right? The opposite also holds true. Children can interpret an absent parent as meaning that they are not a priority or an important part of their parent's life and this belief can be internalised which can lead to poor self-esteem.

Understanding and explaining the difference between self-esteem and self-confidence to your child provides a strong foundation for supporting self-esteem. Self-confidence is about *doing*. The more a child practises something the more confident they can become at a task. It is beneficial to help your child see that self-esteem is NOT about doing but about *being*. Every person is a unique and valuable being in their own right. They deserve respect and love regardless of what they have done in their life or what they look like. Helping a child to see they are loved and valuable *just because they are* and for no other reason is a huge support for their self-esteem. Tying a child's self-worth to what they do in life can harm their self-esteem. Children can come to believe that they are only valuable or only deserve love if they achieve something. Michael Hall discusses this distinction at great length in a later chapter.

A parent who has good self-esteem provides a wonderful role model for their child to follow. By the same token a parent who regularly puts themselves or their child down with language like 'you're so hurtful/stupid/bad/naughty' etc. can harm their child's self-esteem and the child may come to believe those words for life. With our son I focus on talking about his *behaviour* rather than calling him names. For example I might say 'it hurts when you hit someone else. You need to use your words if you're upset with your friends. It's not OK to hit. Just use your words!' In this way he knows his behaviour is hurtful but I have not told him HE is a hurtful or bad child. This is an important distinction as it can make a world of difference to what your children feel and believe about themselves.

2. Health and wellbeing

Life skills in relation to health and wellbeing include improving their understanding in areas like exercise and nutrition, as well as personal and home cleanliness. Children can function more efficiently and effectively in a clean and tidy environment, and diet and exercise play crucial roles in their physical and mental wellbeing. Increasing a child's knowledge of nutrition and how to exercise can reduce the likelihood of childhood obesity and ill health.

Simple activities that can support a child's health and wellbeing include learning about the five food groups. When you prepare a meal you can explain to your children that you chose to include a variety food groups to help them receive optimal nutrition with a balanced diet. You can explain which foods are proteins, carbohydrates, dairy, fruits and vegetables etc. You can also teach your children how to make a healthy after-school snack which helps them to avoid eating foods that are high in sugar and fat.

Alongside a good diet, children need exercise for optimal health and wellbeing. Why not go for a walk with your children on a regular basis to ensure they get their 30 minutes of exercise everyday! My mum, husband and I often go for a walk around our neighbourhood or go to the local park to allow our son to experience time in nature and a place to run, run, run! Enabling your children to participate in team-based sports can support their development of leadership skills, team-playing, goal-setting, calming nerves and developing a healthy lifestyle (Danish 2005).

Finally, you can support your children to develop skills around maintaining order and cleanliness by inviting them to help with the household chores like doing the dishes or taking out the garbage. These activities not only show your children how to clean up but they also help them to take responsibility and understand the importance of contributing as a valuable member of the family.

3. Education, career and money

The *motivation* to learn is an important personal quality, as is the *ability* to learn. Helping children understand the opportunities that effective learning strategies can bring and how learning provides the vehicle for personal and professional development are fundamental to forming a positive attitude to learning at the individual level and a skilled workforce at the national level. The many benefits of higher education for both individuals and society are outlined in a report commissioned by the College Entrance Examination Board (Baum & Payea 2004).

Introducing children to a range of vocations enables younger children to understand how the world works. Moreover, it invites teenagers to consider possible career directions and to seek knowledge about possible fields of specialisation for their future. Personal interests and passion provide children with the motivation to learn. This life skill also explores finances and money as key aspects of everyday life and empowers children with an understanding of the nature and functions of money within society and in their personal lives.

There are a number of ways you can help your child develop life skills around education, career and money including teaching your children how to save. We purchased our son a 'piggy' bank and opened a bank account to teach him about money and savings. We bank and save on his behalf regularly, so that he is able to see that, with each deposit, his savings grow. As he gets older he will understand it more fully but for now he knows he has 'lots of money'. These activities also help your children understand the *value* of money, rather than simply seeing it as a magical unlimited supply that mum and dad get out of the cash machine!

Many children complete secondary education and still don't know the career directions they might like to pursue. By encouraging your child to talk to family members and friends about the advantages and disadvantages of working in a variety of vocations and professions they can develop an idea of the areas they might like to investigate further.

Encourage and nurture your children's inbuilt love of learning by inviting them to go onto the internet and research a topic of interest to them. Then you can ask your children to explain what they have learned to you. This will make them feel valued given they are teaching you something new and it will support their memory and help them practise their recall of the insights they gained by doing the activity.

Is your child organised and productive? Can your child plan and complete activities on time? You can help them learn these valuable life skills. Obtain a diary and show your child how to plan and schedule time for homework, assignments and extra-curricular activities like music lessons and sport training. Make it a daily habit to look in the diary and complete the tasks scheduled for the day. Celebrate the achievements as your child ticks or crosses off the items they've completed.

How do your children view their mistakes or their failures? Do they engage in negative self-talk and give up? For example, would a grade of 47 out of 100 be seen as a failure and result in self-criticism and a negative downward spiral? If so, you can help your children see this grade in a different light – where it simply provides feedback and opportunities to learn and grow as a person. A grade of 47 out of 100 means your child got 47% right and now they only need to work on the 53% they did not! A positive attitude is an important ingredient for life success!

4. Social and environmental understanding

We need to take care of our environment in order to sustain our planet for future generations. For our children to make a positive difference, it's important that they understand how to act ethically and are aware of the social and environmental consequences of their own and other's actions. Social and environmental understanding focuses on developing life skills and personal qualities in relation to the many facets of sustainability. It helps children see that they can choose to make positive contributions in life not just as part of a family, but as a member of a community and a global citizen (Elias and Kress 1994).

You can help your child become a responsible global citizen in many practical ways. It begins by recycling in your home and by taking action locally – such as putting on a pair of gloves, going for a walk down your street with a large garbage bag and picking up the litter in your local area. You can also encourage your children to participate in national clean-up days to expand their awareness of how a nation can work together to make a difference. Inspire your children by sharing stories about individuals like Dr David Suzuki who have spent their lives making a difference globally by educating people about sustaining our planet.

Our son is only three, so we are teaching him the type of rubbish that goes in the 'blue' bin which is the recycling bin and what goes in the 'silver' bin which is waste that goes into landfill. He's pretty good at it now and gets it right most of the time. As he gets older and can understand more, we will also explain *why* he has been doing this, and how recycling and waste impact our planet. It's a step-by-step process and he will gain these life skills as they become age appropriate.

Parents, teachers and other people who come in contact with your children on a regular basis can either help them to build positive character qualities or negative qualities. Positive character qualities include the ability and the desire to act ethically. Providing your children with an introduction to ethics and ethical reasoning skills will help them make the right decisions when faced with ethical dilemmas.

Discussing various ethical dilemmas your children might face gives them an opportunity to explore how they can make good choices and highlight the consequences of poor choices. For example you could ask your child to solve ethical dilemmas like 'if your best friend asks to copy your test paper because they haven't had time to study while taking care of their sick mother, would you let them?' It is helpful to discuss the many alternative choices your child might make and the consequences of each of those choices for everyone involved.

Social awareness is about being conscious of the problems, difficulties or hardships that different people, communities, or societies face on a day-to-day basis. Educating your children in this area will increase their awareness of how others in society live, become more empathetic towards others, think about how they could make a positive difference either now or in the future. It inspires a feeling of gratitude through becoming *aware* of how fortunate they really are. The simple exercise below helps develop your children's understanding about homelessness.

Ask your children to tell you all of the things they usually do in *each* room of your home. For example in the kitchen they can take food from the fridge, cook and enjoy delicious meals. In the bedroom they can sleep, store their clothes and other belongings as well as have a quiet space to relax. In the bathroom they can shower and take care of their personal hygiene. In the family room they can watch TV and so on. Then ask your children to imagine what it is like for a homeless person. Ask them how and where they might cook, store their clothes, wash or sleep. Their reflections will promote social awareness, empathy for others and gratitude for all they have in their lives.

5. Communication skills and relationships

Effective communication skills and an understanding of the dynamics of social relationships are essential life skills. They enable children to develop supportive relationships with family, peers and friends which helps them to work in a productive, harmonious and enjoyable way. Learning how to cooperate and work in a group as well as understanding when to lead and when to follow are valuable skills. Other social skills include understanding how to avoid unnecessary conflict and how to be a good communicator. Building relationships is essential for creating a happy and productive life.

Discovering the complexity of social relationships requires more than just trial and error and a simple understanding of the use of 'manners' and 'protocol'. Communication and social skills need to be developed over time using a comprehensive age-appropriate program of instruction, interaction, experience, reflection and lots of practice. You can try these activities to support your child's development of communication and relationship-building skills.

Help your children understand that communication is about an exchange and so there are times when they can speak and times when they need to listen. It is helpful to role-play different scenarios your children are likely to encounter to give them an opportunity to discover how they can respond and the possible consequences of their words and actions. This is especially important if your child is having difficulty making friends.

Can your children make friends easily? Do your children have the 'right kind' of friends or do they have friends that pressure them into doing things they know they shouldn't do. Help your children identify the qualities they are looking for in a good friend so they are more likely to attract and nurture supportive, rather than harmful, friendships.

Relationships are complex and often people don't actually say what they really mean, so their words don't match their true feelings or thoughts. It's helpful to explain the complex nature of relationships and to invite your child to practise using more than just their ears when they communicate with others. For example, invite them to observe a person's body language and to learn to trust their instinct when they feel a person is not being truthful with them.

Feeling angry is a normal and natural part of life. Things can go wrong and people can get angry! However, some people take their anger out on others and this can destroy relationships. You can help your children manage and express their anger in a way that doesn't hurt others. For example, you can model or encourage your children to walk away from situations if they feel angry in order to take time out and see the situation calmly. Once they have some perspective they can discuss what has upset them with more clarity and less emotion. This is most effective if you model the behaviour when you get angry. In this way your children can actually see how it works! Modelling what *not to do,* with your child seeing the negative consequences of that action, is also a very powerful learning tool if it's accompanied by a discussion of why the behaviour wasn't helpful and an apology to the other person involved. In this way your mistakes become wonderful opportunities for your children to learn that it's OK to make mistakes, the importance of saying sorry and witness the negative effects of poor behaviour on others.

Our son is young and like many young children he can hit or throw things if he gets angry. When I see him do this I help him to develop life skills around managing his emotions and his behaviour. I generally begin by acknowledging his anger rather than ignoring his feelings or reprimanding him. In a firm voice I might say something like 'I can see you are angry, angry, angry.' I then pause for a moment to give him time to see that I've acknowledged his feelings. This usually gets his attention as he feels I *understand*. Then I might say 'please use your words, tell mummy why you're angry. Use your words, mummy is listening, there's no need to hit or throw just use your words!' By working with him in this way, over time he will develop skills for life – to use his words rather than his fists to express his anger.

6. Relaxation and play

In today's society, almost everyone is rushed, overworked, and lacks work and life balance. This is true for our children as well as they are busy with school, homework, sporting activities, after-school tutoring or care, social networking and the list goes on. The development of good life balance begins as a child. This life skill area helps children identify when they are overworked, tired or simply need to rest and provides many techniques for relaxation as well as opportunities to play and have fun. Research shows that most diseases stem from stress! So it is vital to help our children know how to relax and play in order to live a long, happy and healthy life.

Here are some ideas to help your child relax and play. Give your child a shoulder massage and then receive one too. Simply sit your child in a chair, gently rub their shoulders and ask them to relax and enjoy.

After 10–15 minutes ask them to give you a short massage. Touch is such a great way to relax and to bond with your child. Another way you can relax together is to put on some quiet music and lie a bed or on the floor together. For more comfort you can use yoga mats or a blanket on the floor. Then close your eyes, listen to the music and allow it to help you both relax. You could also take some time to stretch with your child. Stretching muscles is great for releasing tension and relaxation.[1] Later in this book, Maggie Dent provides many other practical ideas to helping children manage their stress.

Do your children prefer to play video games and sit at their computers over kicking a ball outside? If you answered yes – you're not alone, many parents say the same about their children. However, playing outside is an important part of a child's wellbeing as a lack of physical activity can lead to obesity; a lack of sunlight can result in vitamin D deficiency; and being in nature can improve a child's attitude towards themselves and the world. Given that playing outside supports children's physical and psychological health, why not plan a picnic in the park. Bring a ball, frisbee or other fun games as well as some healthy food and enjoy the sunshine!

A rainy day? There are lots of ways you can relax and have fun indoors. Play a game of cards or a board game as a family. Invite your child's friends over to play. Get cosy and read a book. Go to the movies. It is all about helping your child understand the benefits of *regularly* taking time out to relax and play for their physical and psychological wellbeing. It's especially important to help them recognise when they are becoming stressed, and to stop and relax before they become really stressed!

7. Inspired creativity

The ability to set and achieve goals are fundamental life skills that will support your child to achieve success in life (Danish et al. 2005). For example, if your child is experiencing a difficulty, having the skills to

---

1 For more ideas see Miller et al. 1991. In this paper they cite a number of other research articles which explore ways to help children manage stress.

clearly identify the source of the problem, the ability to set goals and to feel empowered to take the necessary actions to overcome the difficulty allows your child to turn a challenging situation into a positive one. This helps children feel empowered and encourages them to be resourceful, develop their imaginative skills, discover what inspires them and to take actions to achieve their goals.

To help your child develop life skills in the area of inspired creativity you can try the following activities. Begin by asking your children what goals they'd like to achieve. Encourage them to select a goal that will require a number of steps and some time to achieve. It's good to start with something that can be achieved in a relatively short time to give them a quick success which inspires them to try again. Encourage your children to be specific when identifying their desired outcome, so that they know when they've achieved the goal. For example, rather than a broad goal like 'to lose weight', help them identify a specific and achievable goal like 'to lose two kilograms'.

The next step is to identify the series of action steps that need to be completed in order to achieve the goal. It is also helpful to estimate the time each step will take and to diarise some times that your child can work on the steps. For example, weight loss involves changes in diet and exercise. Schedule in time to exercise for 30 minutes per day and specify the kind of exercise. Also schedule in time to buy and prepare healthy meals and snacks.

Planning is an important part of goal achievement, however, it is the *doing* that will ultimately determine whether the goal will be achieved. Support your children to complete all of the scheduled tasks. Help your children monitor their progress to see if more time is needed and to ensure the goal is achieved. A fun and inspiring part of the process is to recognise and celebrate each of the steps completed, knowing that each action and effort they make will bring them a little closer to achieving their goal! Encourage your children to use their creativity and to stay motivated throughout the process. Later chapters in this book also look at goal setting, so you will have more ideas to work with.

School education

Many parents believe that their children are learning life skills at school. While this is true to some extent, most school programs tend to be focus on study skills and learning curriculum content. A child's development is best supported when life skills are developed *both* in the family home and throughout the primary and secondary school education. This would provide the much needed link and continuity between school and home life for children as well as engage parents in their child's education.

Wouldn't it be wonderful if the school curriculum included a comprehensive program around life skill and personal attribute development? Then school teachers could take the primary responsibility for the life skill development program. This makes sense for many reasons including that children spend more waking hours during the week at school than they do at home, teachers are qualified educators, skilled at supporting children's education and development, and finally the statistics show that family life is so busy with work and home duties that parents and carers have very little time to interact with their children. But until we have a comprehensive school program, the responsibility and of course the pleasure of helping children to develop skills for life will rest with their parents, grandparents and carers.

Helping your child develop key life skills and personal qualities

You can clearly see how important it is for your children to develop life skills and personal qualities to live a happy, healthy and meaningful life. However, you may be wondering *how* you can help them develop these skills. Here are some strategies to support you.

First, the best way to help your children develop life skills is to start as young as possible. Developing life skills doesn't have to be a *chore* – you can make it fun. For example, my toddler loves separating the washing into black, white and colours before he 'stuffs' them in to our front loader washing machine. His favourite part is putting the powder in the drawer and pushing the button. So while he's having fun, he is well on the way to developing a skill for life and there'll be no pink T-shirts for my boy! Starting early makes it a 'normal' part of your children's life which can be continued into the teenage years. As all too many parents of teenagers know if you leave it too late, it is very hard to 'show' them anything!

Second, you need to model the life skills and behaviours you want your children to develop. If you'd like your children to learn the art of calm conflict resolution and negotiation, then model that for them. Children learn from what you do and what you say. How many times have you heard your words come back at you or seen your child do as you have done! So use that to your advantage.

Third, it helps if you have a program of easy to complete activities around developing life skills and work on them regularly. It is most effective if the activities are fun and to become part of your family's weekly routine. In this way, little by little, over time your children learn. As a parent or carer you might be wondering if you have the time and the resources to help your child. The good news is that you don't have to spend a lot of time each week – simply select one or two life skills you'd like to explore with your children each week and then make sure you schedule in some time to develop them.

One or two life skill activities can easily be scheduled into your normal family routine. Developing children's life skills in only 15–20 minutes at a time doesn't sound like much, however, a small amount of focused activity only twice a week means your children can learn up to 104 key life skills and personal attributes in just one year.

Imagine how good you would feel as a parent if your children had good self-esteem and could bounce back when they experience life's difficulties. How happy would you be if your children were able to communicate well, had a close personal relationship with their family and friends and had successful professional relationships? Imagine how proud you'd be if your children had a clear direction and purpose for their life, they loved learning, went out and achieved their goals and gave back to society and the planet.

Parents often feel guilty about not being able to spend as much time as they'd like with their children and everyone who has had a child leave home says 'the time flew by'. Imagine how good you'd feel knowing your child left home with the skills they needed to have a great life!

Further readings and resources

Barrie S (2004). A research-based approach to generic graduate attributes policy. *Higher Education Research & Development*, 23(3): 261–75.

Baum S & Payea K (2005). The benefits of higher education for individuals and society. Education pays 2004. Trends in Higher Education Series. Revised edition. College Entrance Examination Board. Retrieved 1 September 2011 from www.collegeboard.com/prod_downloads/press/cost04/EducationPays2004.pdf.

Botvin G, Griffin K, Paul E & Macaulay A (2003). Preventing tobacco and alcohol use among elementary school students through life skills training. *Journal of Child & Adolescent Substance Abuse*, 12(4): 1–17.

Danish S, Forneris T & Wallace I (2005). Sport-based life skills programming in the schools. *Journal of Applied School Psychology*, 21(2): 41–62.

Elias MJ & Kress JS (1994). Social decision-making and life skills development: a critical thinking approach to health promotion in the middle school. *Journal of School Health*, 64(2): 62–66.

Inspired Children Membership program. Retrieved 1 September 2011 from www.inspiredchildren.com.

Miller S, McCormick J, Lowenstein J, Lang DA, Stinson WJ, Edwards VD, Hofmeier J, Davis R, Ballinger DA & Heine PL (1991). Stress: teaching children to cope. *Journal of Physical Education, Recreation & Dance*, 62(2): 53–70.

Seligman MEP with Reivich K, Jaycox L & Gillham J (1997). *The optimistic child: a proven program to safeguard children against depression and build lifelong resilience.* Boston, New York: Houghton Mifflin Company.

5

Supporting emotional intelligence in children

Dr Joe Dispenza

Imagine what it would have been like if, as a child, you were guided and instructed about how to manage your emotions. Can you see how helpful it would have been to be able to calm yourself, feel balanced and happy instead of feeling stressed, sad or angry for significant parts of your day? Imagine how empowering it would have been as a teenager growing into adulthood to have understood and managed your emotions.

This chapter explores how parents can support the development of their child's emotional intelligence. The chapter has two main aims. The first is to explain *why* helping your child understand and manage their emotions is an incredibly valuable life skill and the second aim is to show you *how* to achieve this. I start with the why, because it makes sense that you would only help your child develop these skills if there were very good reasons for doing so. So let's explore the reasons ...

Emotions: how important are they in life?

Emotions are responses to life experiences. For example, while experiencing a sunset you may feel peaceful. But, if you unexpectedly bump into a previous partner who had wronged you in some way, your response might be to feel anger or betrayal. At a very simple level, as we experience the world, neurons in our brain release chemicals into the body and these chemicals are felt as emotions. There are many, many different kinds of emotions including anger, joy, fear, frustration, happiness, apathy, love, hate, forgiveness, resentment, acceptance, jealousy, indifference, ecstasy and the list goes on ... too many to mention here, but you're getting a feel for what I'm talking about, right? While there are many different kinds of emotions, at a very broad level, they can all be classified into one of three categories, namely: positive emotions like happiness, joy and love; negative emotions like hate, anger and jealousy; or neutral emotions like acceptance or indifference.

Have you ever stopped to wonder what role these complex and multifaceted positive, negative and neutral emotions play in your life? Here are some common life circumstances for you to consider to help you answer this question for yourself.

- Have you ever felt really angry and said or done things that, once you calmed down, you wished you had never said or done?
- Have you noticed that whatever is happening in your life can quite often influence your emotions in a positive or negative way? For example, if everything flows on your way to work you're in a good mood and have a good day, but if you spill coffee on yourself, miss the train or get caught in traffic it puts you in a bad mood and you feel that you've had a bad start to the day!
- Have you ever taken the time to say a kind word to someone in need which helped them feel so much better and made a positive difference in their life?
- When you are feeling positive or in a good mood, have you ever noticed how many wonderful opportunities appear in your life and how much more motivated you are to do things?
- Have you ever noticed that when you are in a critical mood, how many other critical people appear – ready to criticise and complain with you?
- If you happen to be in a bad mood, have you ever found that if something negative comes up unexpectedly, that you are not as resilient as when you are feeling up? Have you ever noticed that when you are feeling down, the occurrence of a negative circumstance is more likely to make you feel that it is unfair, to wonder why is it always you that bad things happen to and to believe that you can't cope? On the other hand, do you find that if you are feeling good, something going wrong is manageable and doesn't seem so important?

- Have you ever experienced the clarity in your thoughts and the ease with which you can make a decision when you feel acceptance?
- Have you noticed that sometimes a really small thing can make you feel instantly angry or frustrated? For example, when you are in a hurry, have you ever become enraged by the lights changing to red or the traffic moving too slowly or even worse still, someone cutting in front of you on the road? Have you experienced a Dr Jekyll and Mr Hyde kind of moment?
- Have you ever felt so bad that you either have, or have wanted to, hurt yourself or someone else?
- Have you ever noticed that if you feel frustrated and your child comes up to you and wants your time and energy how short tempered and dismissive you can be?
- Has someone ever made a negative comment about you that has left you feeling devastated?
- Have you ever felt so fearful that you were paralysed and couldn't speak or act?
- Have you ever stopped to wonder how quickly a positive thought can make you feel great and equally how quickly a negative thought can make you feel down?

Based on these few common life experiences, can you see that our emotions affect how we see and interpret the world as well as how we respond or behave in the world and therefore our emotions affect every part of our lives? Let's explore this a little further by drawing on the findings of scientific research.

Studies at the University of Pennsylvania have reported that if you show two different pictures in rapid succession, one from a funeral scene and one from a feast scene to a group of depressed people, when asked which they remember, the depressed people remember the coffin scene at percentages greater than chance. That is, they perceived their environment which then continuously reinforces how they feel – depressed (Beck 1976). How these findings translate into everyday life is that, in general, people who are depressed focus on the negative things in their lives which then keep them feeling depressed. It seems that people who are depressed take less notice, or even completely miss the good things in life which could take them out of depression. This study clearly shows that people perceive reality based on how they feel, so their emotions colour their perceptions of the world. Have you ever wondered how your negative emotional states affect what you focus on in your life and what opportunities you might be missing?

Our emotions not only affect how we *see* and *interpret* the world, they can also affect how we *act* or *behave* in the world. Have you ever noticed that: if you are feeling apathetic you find it difficult to take action; if you are feeling angry you are more likely to say and do hurtful things; and if you are feeling joy or love you are more likely to act selflessly? In other words, your emotions tend to influence your behaviours.

If you accept that your emotions can play a significant role in how you see your life and how you behave, have you considered how much you know about your emotions, how much control you have over your emotions or whether in fact your emotions control you?

Different kinds of emotional predispositions

While it is certainly true that each person is unique and each person will experience a variety of different emotions throughout their day, people also have a tendency or predisposition towards a dominant emotional experience. A number of different kinds of emotional dispositions are described below. Take a moment to read them and where you can, try to match each case with someone you know. Also, identify which emotional propensity most resembles you. These examples might seem to be overgeneralisations, but try the exercise anyway to see what it shows you …

Who in your life generally expresses themselves in the world like this?

- *Happy* disposition where the person generally sees the good in any situation.
- *Depressed* disposition where the person generally feels down and critical of themselves most of the time despite any good aspects in their life.
- A disposition of *self-pity* which can express itself as 'everyone is

better off, no-one looks after me, everyone is more important than me, everything aches and pains, nothing seems to go right for me'.

- *Balanced* emotional disposition, nothing seems to faze these people and they tend to go with the flow of life. They accept change, adapt and cope so they are generally happy, easygoing people.
- *Psychotic* or 'touchy' emotional disposition where the person can be calm one minute and the next, for very little or even no apparent reason, they exhibit angry, blaming and aggressive emotions.
- *Apathetic* emotional disposition where nothing, not even a great amount of effort from others, can get them to feel motivated and positive about their life.
- *Fun-loving* disposition which generally manifests itself as not taking responsibility for anything, possibly reckless behaviour and only doing things that nurture their desire to maintain their fun emotional state.
- Emotionally *changeable* disposition – sometimes up, sometimes down and sometimes indifferent. Emotions change in response to the external environment.
- Emotionally *measured* disposition where, no matter what, these people do not express any emotion and always appear unemotional or neutral. Stereotypical accountants are often categorised here.
- *Sad* disposition where the person can't seem to find any joy in their life.
- *Fearful* disposition where the person lives with a feeling of fear for most of their day. They may be unable to act in the world as their fear paralyses them.
- *Bored* disposition, which is often associated with unmotivated teenage boys! You hear words like 'I'm bored, that's boring, and everything is boring, snore, snore ... zzz ...'
- *Angry* disposition where the person generally feels angry at themselves, others and the world. Any small thing can set them off into a rage.

Are there any other common emotional dispositions you can think of?

Were you able to identify at least one person for each of the above categories? Which category, if any, are you predominately in? You might be wondering why this is important and how this relates to the first aim of the chapter, namely to explain why helping your child manage their emotions is so important … stay with me … it will become clear soon.

We already know that each person is unique and will experience a variety of different emotions throughout their day. However, if we also accept that each person has a predisposition or a propensity towards a dominant emotional experience, then, it is important to consider the effects of these emotional predispositions on a person's life.[1] At the simplest level of analysis, which of the emotional dispositions listed above do you believe will help a person live a fulfilling, happy and productive life? Which dispositions do you believe are more likely to result in a person living a difficult, unproductive and unhappy life? This is not meant to be a trick question. The answer is obvious – it doesn't take a genius to know that a happy disposition is more likely to be supportive for leading a happy and fulfilling life, and dispositions based on anger, self-pity or depression are less likely to be life-enabling.

If emotional predispositions are so important, then if we are to direct our lives in the best way, it makes sense that we need to have a good understanding of our emotions, our emotional predispositions and more importantly we need to be able to control our emotions as opposed to allowing our emotions to control us. So, if a happy emotional disposition is the most life-enabling, why then, don't we ALL CHOOSE to live from a happy emotional disposition?

Emotional predispositions are the result of both our genes (nature) and our experiences (nurture). For example, let's say a child is born to parents who have angry emotional dispositions. The child is likely to be born with a genetic angry emotional predisposition. If all they experience is anger and rage in their external environment as they grow up, then they are likely to have an angry emotional disposition. If on the other hand, that same child was adopted into a calm, gentle and nurturing family after it was born, then it is possible for that child to

---

1 Dominant emotional predispositions can also be called personality traits. Discussed later in the chapter.

develop a calm emotional disposition based on their experiences and responses to the nurturing environment despite the genetic predisposition. This means that emotional predispositions are the result of the interplay between our genetics (nature) and the environments we grow up in (nurture). In chapter two, Bruce Lipton explored how parents can positively influence their child's genetic predispositions by modifying their own behaviour before conception. In chapter three, Monique Robinson explained how mothers who are overly stressed during pregnancy are more likely to have babies who have dysfunctional emotional and behavioral predispositions including hyperactivity and attention deficit syndrome. In this chapter, the focus is on the 'nurture' aspect of the process, that is, how our responses to our environment can influence our emotional predispositions.

How emotional predispositions develop: environmental responses

Emotional predispositions develop as a result of a series of processes that take place within our body that occur consistently over time. They do not happen overnight, they develop over time as a result of our repetitive responses to the external world. While these processes are complex, they can be simplified in order to make them easier to understand. Let's start with our thinking.

Every time a person has a thought they make chemicals in their brain which are released into the body. A person may have happy and empowering thoughts as their response to an experience, and in a matter of seconds they will produce chemicals that make them feel empowered and happy. On the other hand, self-deprecating, negative, sad or angry thoughts produce chemicals that make a person feel sad, angry or depressed. Perhaps you've experienced how quickly your thoughts can affect your emotions. So, basically the first step in the process of developing emotional predispositions is that the 'immaterial thing' we called a thought, which is our response to the environment, causes the brain to release chemicals so that our body feels exactly the same way we are currently thinking.

These processes are best explained using a specific example. Let's assume that a person has failed an exam and has negative self-deprecating thoughts like 'I'm stupid, I'll never amount to anything or I'm hopeless at everything ...' and their brain has released chemicals into their body and so now the person feels depressed. When a person's thinking and feelings are aligned, this is called a state of being. The next step in the process is that, among many other things, the brain is always monitoring and evaluating the body's internal environment, which includes evaluating how the body is feeling as a result of the chemicals that have been released. So in this case, the brain notices that the body is feeling depressed and so the brain then tends to think the way the body feels, which then results in the brain making more chemicals so that the body continues to feel the way the brain is thinking and so on and so on resulting in a sustained period of chemical continuity. Therefore a negative thought creates negative emotions which create more negative thoughts which create more negative emotions until the person creates a sustained negative emotional reaction or a sustained state of being. In this case, the person is feeling really depressed!

It is important to understand that there is nothing wrong with having a negative or a positive emotional reaction and that negative emotional reactions do not automatically result in negative emotional predispositions. A negative emotional reaction is quite normal under a variety of life circumstances and even the happiest of people can sometimes feel sad and depressed. An emotional predisposition does not develop as a result of one negative emotional incident but instead develops as a result of a series of processes that take place within our body that occur consistently over time and these processes can go on for days, weeks, months or even years on end.

To explain further, after a person has a thought chemicals are released into their body creating an emotional reaction to match the thought. Just after this occurs, there is a period called the refractory period. This is a small space in time after the emotional reaction in which a person can make a number of choices about what happens next. They might:

- Attempt to change their state of being and return to a state of calm by noticing the reaction, stopping everything for a moment and simply observing their emotional state. The person may calm themselves by taking a breath, walking away or having a glass of water.

- Consciously initiate positive thoughts which will release chemicals that invoke positive emotions which can break the cycle of negative thoughts and negative emotions. For example, the person may notice the self-deprecating thought and replace it with a self-empowering thought.
- Initiate more negative thoughts releasing more chemicals that lead to more negative emotions, which then sustains the negative state of being and extends the refractory period.

If this refractory period is further extended by the person continuing the cycle of negative thoughts which release chemicals that lead to negative emotions which only lead to more negative thoughts, it can become a self-perpetuating cycle fuelled and reinforced by negative thoughts and emotions. The cycle of negative thinking and feeling moves the person out of the refractory period and into a state of chemical continuity creating an emotional predisposition.

To illustrate with an example, if a person keeps an angry emotional reaction going for hours or even days it's called a 'mood'. It's very common for people to be in a sad, happy or angry mood from time to time, right? In this case no permanent harm is done as the emotional reaction comes, and then reasonably soon after, it goes. On the other hand, if a person keeps an angry mood going for weeks or months it's called a 'temperament'. This is where we start to get to a potentially harmful part in the process, because if a person keeps this temperament running for months or years then that's called an emotional predisposition or a personality trait. Therefore, our emotional predispositions or personality traits are created from our persistent emotional reactions based on the chemical continuity of the self-perpetuating thinking/feeling cycle.

When a person perpetuates the same negative thoughts and the same negative emotional reactions over and over again, then they become very good at it and become conditioned to that emotion. They become like an expert with that emotional reaction and that kind of thinking and it becomes their natural state of being – or emotional predisposition. It becomes programmed into the subconscious and it becomes an automatic process.[2] Once this occurs, the person has little or no conscious control over their emotional reaction and that is why people can't simply choose not to go with their natural predisposition – it is who they have become – it is who they are!

This is similar to the processes that Bruce Lipton described in chapter two, when he explained how the approach to parenting you experienced as a child generally becomes programmed into your genes which then becomes the automatic way you behave as a parent and the genes you pass on to your own children, unless of course you consciously change that subconscious parenting programming and your genetic expression before conception.

Once a person becomes conditioned to an emotional reaction, change is a difficult process. It is like you are trying to 'unlearn' how to drive a car after you have been driving for years! As soon as you sit in the car you know what to do and you do it automatically. It is the same for an emotional predisposition. For example, a person with an angry predisposition will tend to automatically respond to most situations in an angry way. They can't help it as it is predominantly out of their control. Once a predisposition is in place, it takes a great act of will, mindfulness and a huge effort to act differently, to be different and to change!

---

2 The conditioning happens as the body and mind re-experience the emotions and thoughts associated with an event for an extended period of time. The event may actually be happening in their life over and over again triggering the thoughts and emotions or the event could simply be replayed in the person's mind and body *long after* the actual event occurred. This occurs with post traumatic stress syndrome. The body acts as if the event is still actually happening and it feels real when it is not actually real in this moment! Once the body has been conditioned to expect those feelings it is then able to rule the mind, as the feelings in the body become stronger than the logical mind. In other words, the fear experienced in the body is stronger than the logical mind which should 'know' that there is no threat. Unfortunately, the mind simply responds with fearful thoughts based on the strong fearful feelings in the body which fuels the chemical continuity in the body.

To make the explanation even more realistic, we can take the discussion one step further using another analogy, that of smoking. After a person has been smoking cigarettes for some time their body becomes addicted to the chemicals in the cigarettes. In the same way, when a person continually thinks negative thoughts which then continually bathes their body in negative emotional chemicals, their body becomes addicted to those negative chemicals and it craves them just as a smoker craves nicotine. So when the chemicals start to decrease, then the body itself sends a signal to the mind in order to invoke more negative thoughts so that more negative chemicals are created to satisfy the craving and to perpetuate the negative feeling ... is this sounding scary? If you answered yes – you are right and there's even more!

Can you recall thinking about something negative that might happen in the future and feeling anxious about it even thought it isn't actually happening? For example, have you thought the worst when the phone rings late at night and felt scared that something has happened to your children? Have you felt paralysed with fear at the mere thought of having to speak publicly? You might have noticed that your feelings felt real – like you were actually experiencing the event in that moment, however your body had the experience by thought alone and it wasn't real at all. Your body didn't distinguish between really experiencing it and experiencing it simply because you thought something bad happened. If danger is really happening, then automatic responses are adaptive and helpful. If you have someone running after you to attack you, then feeling fear and running away is very good. However, imagining or replaying this scenario in your mind, time and time again then experiencing the fear over and over again is obviously maladaptive and harmful for the body and to your quality of life!

Now it is time to bring the discussion back to parenting and to explain why helping your children to develop emotional intelligence is so important. Are you starting to see that we need to help our children understand and manage their emotions so that they don't develop negative emotional predispositions by perpetuating negative thinking and negative feeling cycles that will have a negative impact on their perceptions of, and actions taken in their lives? Further, are you starting to see how important it would be to help our children actively work towards developing life enhancing positive emotional predispositions? If you can now see *why* it is important to help your children manage their emotions and emotional predispositions, then you are ready to learn about *how* to do it and we move onto the second aim of this chapter!

Developing emotional intelligence

The concept of emotional intelligence was first proposed by Peter Salovey and John D. Mayer in 1990. Sometime later, it was further developed and became widely known through Daniel Goleman's bestselling book *Emotional intelligence* (1995). While this chapter is not directly based on this work, it draws on their insightful working definition of emotional intelligence. These authors outline five distinct but interrelated aspects (or as they call them domains) of emotional intelligence. Identifying these unique aspects is helpful when attempting to unravel and explain in a simple way, the complex concept of emotional intelligence. The five aspects of emotional intelligence are:

- *knowing one's emotions* – this aspect is about being aware of your emotions as they are happening
- *managing emotions* – this aspect is about handling and changing your emotions, being able to shake off negative emotions and introduce positive emotions
- *recognising emotions in others* – this aspect is about empathy and being aware of other's needs
- *handling relationships* – this aspect is about interpersonal effectiveness and interacting with others
- *motivating oneself* – this aspect is about being able to work towards a goal, being able to get into the flow to achieve outstanding performance.

It is important to note that while these five aspects are identified as separate aspects of emotional intelligence, they are interconnected. Both the unique and the interrelated parts of the first four aspects of emotional intelligence are discussed in the remainder of this chapter, and motivating oneself is discussed in later chapters.

Knowing your emotions is about being aware of your emotions as they are happening. This is about being able to observe yourself. Most of the time when we are experiencing an emotion, we are not aware of it. We are so immersed in the experience that we are the experience and no part of us is outside the experience to be aware or observe the experience. However, perhaps you have experienced from time to time that you have noticed that you are immersed in an emotion such as anger, sadness, self-pity or jealously. In that moment of awareness, you are both in the emotion and separate from it as well ... there is something observing you and that something is the frontal lobe of your brain – this is the part of the brain that enables consciousness and supports you to achieve a state of balance again. So, the first aspect of emotional intelligence is about developing the ability to be aware of your emotions while you are experiencing them.

Why is awareness valuable?

Have you ever observed an argument between two people who are angry at each other and witnessed the irrational and hurtful things they say while they are immersed in emotions of anger, hurt or hate? Have you ever reflected on how they could have handled the situation so much better if they were calm and were able to hear each other and sort it out in a more caring way? Now, have you ever said things in anger that you wished you'd never said and wondered where those words came from – they just seemed to fly out of your mouth before you could think about them or stop them? This happens as we have no control when we are immersed in a negative emotion because we revert to the subconscious part of our brain where the automatic programs reside.

When we are immersed in an emotion like anger we revert to a primitive part of the brain called the midbrain which is all about survival – fight or flight. This brain doesn't have the higher intelligence of our frontal lobe so we are relying on an outdated – and I mean really primitive – part of our brain to operate in the world. As you have probably seen yourself time and time again, when you are immersed in a negative emotion and you are operating solely from that primitive brain you say things and do things that later when you are calm and thinking from the frontal lobe of your brain with conscious intelligence, you wished you'd never said or done. In other words when you are NOT in a life-threatening experience, you almost always DO NOT make good decisions when you are immersed in a negative emotion and operate from a primitive cave person mentality!

However, this primitive part of the brain plays an essential role in our lives in times when there is a real physical threat. For example, if we are walking across the road and a bus is heading for us, then we don't want our frontal lobe coming in and having a discussion with ourselves about what is happening here and what we should do, because if we did that we would probably be squashed in the middle of the road. In a life-threatening situation the primitive brain automatically steps in, and in this case our body will automatically choose flight and move out of the path of the bus! So we need the primitive brain for life-threatening situations and we need to work with the higher intelligence of our frontal lobe in all other situations.

Now, what if you could be aware of your emotions as they were happening? Wouldn't it make a huge difference if when you noticed you were feeling negative emotions such as fear, anger, hate or jealously, you could say to yourself:

> Oh no … cave person is here … stop … leave the situation now before you say anything stupid or say something you will regret later … OK … breathe … calm yourself … you know you never say anything sensible when you are really angry … remember this is not a life-threatening situation.

Imagine then, if you listened to yourself and if you didn't say anything or do anything until you had time to calm yourself, consider the situation and talk with care and compassion and real intelligence for a win/win situation? Obviously this is the way to go … imagine how different your day, week and life would be if everyone acted this way. The world would truly be a different place.

If we are to make this happen, we have to start with ourselves in order to role model and help our children find a new way to interact with people by operating with emotional intelligence. The first aspect of emotional intelligence is to be aware of your negative emotions as you are experiencing them in order for you to have choice over whether to continue with them or change them!

So how can we teach our children (and ourselves for that matter) emotional awareness? I have helped my children develop this skill in two main ways and I began the learning process when they were very young, when they were toddlers. One strategy I used was to observe my children when they were immersed in a negative emotional experience such as fighting over a toy. A second strategy was to play games in order for my children to learn about, and to consciously experience, different emotions. These two strategies are explored below in more detail.

Parental observation

As a parent you witness your child's numerous emotional experiences. Many times you observe the joy and happiness they experience as they learn, grow and play in the world. However, as a natural part of growing up, children will also experience many negative emotions such as frustration, anger and jealousy. It may occur if they feel frustrated that they can't say or do something they want to and they may express their frustration by throwing themselves on the floor, screaming and writhing about as if possessed! Emotions of anger may arise if they fight with a sibling or friend over a toy where they get angry and even hit or bite. Whichever way it manifests, it is as unpleasant for your child as it is for you! Remember, a negative thought releases chemicals to make the body feel negative and that is what your child is experiencing! Poor thing!

OK, so what now? This situation is usually very uncomfortable for a parent and so the instinctive reaction is to get in there and sort it out. However, I didn't do this when my children were growing up as I believe it's not as helpful as saying something very simple like 'you seem angry' in a calm non-judgmental tone which helps them to become aware of their state and detach from the emotion. I'd walk away once I could see they were OK. Another technique I often used was to simply observe them in a calm and loving way. When I saw my children fighting with each other or their friends, as long as they were not in real danger of hurting themselves or each other, I would make my presence known by observing them. I would watch them, without judgment, until they were aware that I was watching them. I would observe for a moment, and this interruption to their emotional outburst gave them space, which allowed them to become aware that someone was watching them and they then had the opportunity to observe their own emotions and behaviour. At this stage I would rarely say anything but after I had observed them for some time, and they observed me observing them, and they were aware of themselves, I would simply go back to whatever I was doing. On some occasions I would have to repeat this many times … depending on how many times they went into negative emotional reactions. On other occasions, one or more of my children would come over to me for comfort, I would, of course hold them to comfort them but I still would not say much, if anything at all.

You might be wondering why I didn't say anything and why I didn't use this as a teaching moment. My first rule is never to reason with a child when they are emotional as they are not in a state conducive for learning. You know for yourself that when you're all worked up you're generally not receptive, right? So what I do to help my children learn is explained in the pages to come when I discuss the other aspects of emotional intelligence including, managing emotions, recognising emotions in others, and handling relationships. The focus here is on the 'knowing one's emotions' aspect of emotional intelligence which is purely about being aware of your emotions when you are in the emotion. My intention is for my children to become aware of themselves and their emotional state by noticing that I am observing them. This helps them to become aware of themselves which breaks the thinking-feeling cycle for a moment. This is one way you can help your child develop the ability to observe their own emotions. The second way is to help them become more familiar with their emotions by intentionally playing games that explore emotions. In this way, your child becomes familiar with the emotions and how they manifest in their body which means they are more likely to be aware of their emotions when they arise.

Playing games to learn about emotions

In your life you have probably seen hundreds of movies. Have you noticed that actors have the ability to bring up any emotion at will? In a horror movie they need to feel and look scared! In a love story they need to be able to feel love and passion to carry the scene and make it look realistic. When someone dies, they need to be able to cry and feel sad. If they could not bring these emotions to life at will, the movie would be a 'flop' as it wouldn't look realistic!

The ability to bring up any emotion on demand is called emotional plasticity and it is not only a wonderful life skill for actors, it is a powerful skill for managing all aspects of your life effectively. To be able to be aware of and understand an emotion, your child needs to experience it. This can be achieved in a really simple and fun way.

The way I did it was to take any opportunity we were together to help my children learn about emotional intelligence. For example, let's say we were driving in the car. I would play a fun game where we would all explore and rehearse different emotions together. I might begin the game by saying:

> OK, let's play a game and the game involves us all feeling happy for the next five minutes, so everybody stay in a state of joy, think about what makes you feel happy and then really feel it … notice how it makes you feel inside … you may feel like smiling, you may feel light … you may even feel like you are bursting with excitement because you are so happy … notice that feeling … make that feeling grow so you are even more happy … keep the feeling of happiness and joy …

Now when the five minutes were up I would say '… now memorise that feeling of happiness and joy, come on memorise it, because that is who you really are …' The reason I said this was to help my children to develop the habit of happiness and to be happy. My children can develop a happy emotional predisposition when happiness is programmed into their subconscious and they automatically operate from a place of happiness in the world. They are then truly being happy. Let's face it, who doesn't want their child to be happy? Obviously helping your child to live from a place of happiness is so much better than your child automatically operating from a place of fear or anger when interacting in the world!

Then for the rest of the car journey I would ask my children to pick emotions that they wanted to explore. One child may say I want to be strong so I'd help by guiding them to really feel the feeling, so that they would know that feeling in themselves, recognise it and even call upon it when they need it in their life. For example I might say:

> OK, let's all feel strong for the next five minutes, everybody stay in a state of strength and feeling powerful, think about what makes you feel strong and then really feel it ... notice how it makes you feel inside ... you may feel like you are walking tall, you may feel like your chest is swelling and your heart is growing the courage of a lion ... you may even feel like you are bursting with strength because you are invincible, you are able to do anything, you are so brave and strong ... notice that feeling ... make that feeling even stronger ... keep the feeling of strength and courage ... now memorise that feeling of being strong and invincible, come on memorise it, because that is who you really are ...

Other positive emotions we explored included: feeling free like a cloud, feeling angelic, feeling still, calm and quiet or feeling like laughing. Now this little activity of 'playing with and rehearsing emotions' could go on for the whole trip or for the time the children were willing to participate. It lasted while ever it was fun and the children were enjoying it and were learning to be emotionally versatile. Once it was no longer of interest, we did something else. It is important not to *force* the game ... a game has to be fun and children learn the most when they are having fun! Like most things in life, practice makes perfect. Helping children develop the ability to 'call up' positive thoughts and emotions easily is such a valuable tool as they can use this to change their own state of being. If they notice they're feeling a bit low, they can shorten the period of feeling down (refractory period) by proactively changing their state of being with positive thoughts and then experiencing positive emotions – now that's emotional intelligence!

It is also important to allow your children to experience, to be able to recognise and to be able to bring up negative emotions. When playing a game exploring negative emotions it is more about learning about how the negative emotions feel in their body rather than helping them to actually experience them at a deep level for prolonged periods. It is more about helping your child notice how negative emotions make them feel inside. For example they may feel unhappy, angry, frustrated, or their muscles may feel tight, or they may feel heavy, or their tummy may feel upset, or their body may feel hot and how they will generally feel bad inside. Again it is about helping children know what the emotions feel like so they can recognise them when they arise. No doubt your children will provide themselves with lots of opportunities to experience negative emotions without your help!

To sum up, the first part of emotional intelligence is about developing an awareness of emotions while experiencing them. The two exercises described above can help your child with this skill. First they need to be able to experience and really know the many different positive and negative emotions a person can experience so play the 'lets all feel XX' game when appropriate. Second, with your help your child needs to be able to observe themselves while experiencing an emotional state. You can help them develop this awareness by observing your child when you see the opportunity arise, by allowing them to observe you observing them. It is also very important and extremely helpful to talk to your child about the idea of observing their own emotional states and how and why you do it in your life. You can create games for them to play like 'catch my emotions'. In this game every time your child notices a change in their emotions they can write it in a journal or perhaps they could draw a smiley face, sad face or angry face on the calendar depending on which emotion they notice. The journal and calendar become something you can reflect upon and talk about and use as a learning tool. You can probably create other activities – just be imaginative and experiment. Over time each of these activities and processes will help your child develop the knowing one's emotions aspect of emotional intelligence. Once a child can see and be aware of their emotions the next thing is to be able to manage them.

Managing emotions

The managing emotions aspect of emotional intelligence is about handling and changing your emotions, being able to shake off negative emotions and introduce positive emotions once you recognise you have them.

In the section above we talked about how we can help children introduce positive emotions at will. It is also important that children explore the darker or negative emotions and learn how to manage them. Children need to explore and understand anger, frustration, hate, jealousy, apathy, depression and all other negative emotions that they will experience in their lives and see others experience. I never told my children to suppress their emotions. I encouraged them to express their emotions as I wanted them to get them all out and didn't want the suppressed emotions to be stuck in their bodies! However, it was just as important to help them get over their negative emotional expressions quickly, as I didn't want them to practise and become experts at negative emotions and develop a negative emotional predisposition. In a light hearted way I would say to my children, 'if you are angry for more than 20 minutes you're faking it. You can't be angry for that long … you must be getting addicted to that emotion'. Remember the discussion earlier in the chapter which explained how emotional predispositions and personality traits arise from a series of processes that take place within our body that occur consistently over time. In other words, the self-perpetuating cycle of negative thoughts releasing chemicals that lead to negative emotions which only lead to more negative thoughts in a self-perpetuating cycle continually fuelling and reinforcing negative emotions and which will eventually result in more permanent, negative emotional predispositions. This is NOT what you want for your child. Right?

On the other hand, the exercises and fun activities we design for our children which help them understand and create positive emotions that they can practice over and over again, will result in positive subconscious programs and ways of being in the world which will empower their lives. So we want that … right again!

How can we teach our children to manage their emotions?

The way I did it was to share how I was working with managing my emotions – that is, I modelled the process for them as well as coached them through managing their own emotions. Developing emotional intelligence is an ongoing life time process and as a family, we're all becoming more able to manage our emotions as time goes on.

OK, how did the process work for my family? Let's say my children were playing together in another room and they got into an argument over a toy. They might be shouting and arguing and even pushing and pulling the toy and each other, so I would come into the room and stand in the doorway and observe them. If no one was in any real harm, I wouldn't intervene I would just wait at the door and watch them until they noticed me watching them. I wouldn't say anything. I simply waited for them to notice me, then to become aware of the situation, so that they could become aware of their own emotions. Once my children appeared to have settled down I'd walk out and resume what I was doing.

I didn't try and reason with or help my child learn something at that time because when a child is in a highly negative emotional state they can't be reasoned with and therefore they can't learn. Remember the discussion on the primitive brain – they are operating from the subconscious primitive brain, not the more conscious frontal lobe, and so that can't reflect and learn anything when they are in that state. Think about this: can someone reason with you when you are really angry or frustrated? Can you hear reason, are you even open to listening when you are angry? The answer is usually NO. Well it's the same with your children. So rule number one in relation to teaching your children about managing their emotions is NOT to try to teach them anything when they are still very much immersed in the emotion.

However, much later, just before bed, when the conscious mind is slowing down at the end of the day and the subconscious mind is beginning to open, is when I help my children learn about how to manage their emotions. The process I am about to describe actually encompasses a number of the aspects of emotional intelligence including managing emotions, recognising emotions in others as well as handling relationships.

Teaching children to manage emotions, recognise emotions in others and handle relationships

Every night I lie on the bed with my children and we talk and reflect on our day. I use this time to share and connect with my children as well as to help them develop the ability to manage their emotions and behaviours. Before bed is a good time to support their development as the subconscious mind opens up twice during the day – once in the early morning and again in the evening when the body is winding down for sleep. These times are the most powerful times for getting information into the subconscious part of your child's brain.

Most of the time, I would start our conversations by sharing the emotions I have experienced and explored that day. For example I might say something along the lines; you know today I was working with my anger. I was driving the car and I was in a hurry to get home and the lights changed to red and I had to stop. And you know I started to feel hot and fidgety inside and I was really getting impatient. Then I noticed that when I feel impatient I also feel angry and that brings up other emotions like I was being really judgmental. So when I saw people crossing the road in front of me I noticed that I started being critical towards them and I didn't even know these people. I was thinking 'I don't like the way you look or how you are walking or I don't like you' and that didn't make sense because I didn't even know them. Most importantly I realised I felt really bad inside.

But then I remembered that I have control over my own emotions and that I was working with being aware of my anger and other negative emotions. I knew that I hadn't failed because I remembered – I caught myself before I let the negative emotions go on too long. Then I said to myself 'now that you have remembered, now that you have seen yourself get angry, you can choose to feel something different, to feel something more positive.' So I decided to be happy instead of angry because happy feels so much better than angry and judgmental. I realised that I didn't have any control over when the traffic lights would change or how fast the traffic will flow but I do have control over my emotions. I remembered how we played the game in the car where we all felt happy and strong, and remembered how good those emotions felt. I thought about all of the things I am so grateful for and I said them in my mind 'I am so grateful for my kids, for my home, for my family's health and for the family vacation we went on last month – they all make me feel happy'. I realised that I felt so much better, I was feeling happy now as I'd stopped myself from feeling angry and I said 'ah this feels so good!' After I had finished describing my day, I would stop and say nothing more in order to give my children some time to contemplate what I'd just shared with them. By sharing my own emotional development I am both modelling how to do it, as well as building a relationship of openness and trust with my children.

After I finished my story, more often than not one of the children would say something along the lines of 'you know what dad? I was working with anger today too'. If I was there and witnessed it I would say 'yes, I saw you! Can you tell me about it'? Otherwise, if I hadn't seen the incident, I would ask them to tell me all about it. They might express how they had been playing together and that at some point in time they both wanted the same toy and then they got so angry they pulled the toy away from each other and some nasty words were said and then one got so angry they wanted to hit the other … and so on. You can see that my child is now being reflective through the process of recalling and re-telling the incident. Once the whole story is retold, we would begin a collaborative effort to discover new ways to deal with the situation in a positive way. I would begin by asking my child:

> Now that you know what happens if you argue over a toy and act in the way you did, if you had that same experience again, how could you do it differently so that there is a better outcome where you both didn't feel so bad?

My child would often make some suggestions based on their childlike view of the world and their limited experiences and so I would help them expand their view and reflect on the consequences of their suggestions, in this way the process was collaborative. The whole conversation was from a place of love, caring, learning, exploration, exchange and most importantly acceptance and non judgement. So let's say my child suggested 'well what I could do is hide that toy in my room and only play with it when my brother isn't around and then we wouldn't fight about it'. Then I would say something like:

> Dad: Well if you did that, then you would be playing by yourself and you wouldn't learn about sharing and you wouldn't have a chance to practise sharing so you wouldn't have the fun experiences that you have when you play with someone else. Have you thought about that?'
>
> Child: Hmm, no dad, I didn't think about that.
>
> Dad: You might also find that based on your choice not to share your toys that your brother also decides not to share his toys with you and then you would only have your toys to play with. Have you thought about that?
>
> Child: Hmm, no dad, I didn't think about that either.
>
> Dad: Instead of worrying about the toy, did you think about your brother's feelings if you don't share? Did you think about how much you like your brother and how good it feels to have fun playing with him and how you don't want to hurt his feelings?
>
> Child: Hmm, no dad, I didn't think about that either.
>
> Dad: OK, can you think about something else you could do …

This process goes on until they have exhausted all of their options and they are ready to hear some other ideas they might try. The conversation might go like this:

> Dad: Well what about this idea. How about if this happens again that first you try to notice that you are getting angry and you stop for a moment. Maybe you could take a few deep breaths or go for a walk outside, think about things that make you happy or lie down and relax for a minute until you don't feel angry anymore. Because you know that you have better ideas when you are happy, then you could think about how you could find a solution where both you and your brother would be happy. How does that sound?
>
> Child: OK dad, I can try it.

Dad: If a situation came up where you both wanted to play with one toy, could you suggest that you each take a turn for 5–10 minutes and then toss a coin for who goes first? Do you think that would be a good outcome for both you and your brother? Do you think it would be helpful for keeping your good relationship with your brother? How does that sound?

Child: OK sounds good, dad. I can try it.

Notice that in this little exercise, my child has learned something about the importance of being aware of her emotions while they are occurring, managing her own emotions, being aware of another's emotions and handling relationships in a positive way. This covers the first four aspects of emotional intelligence as defined earlier in the chapter. Imagine how much your child could learn about emotional intelligence if you did this on a regular basis? Month by month, year by year – as is age appropriate – you can help your child develop their emotional intelligence by stretching them a little more and co-developing more and more sophisticated solutions for them to try in the world.

Once you have explored each situation together and come up with some agreed helpful options your child can try if the situation comes about again, the next step in the process is to help your child REMEMBER what they have just learned and more importantly to be able to BEHAVE in a new way when a similar situation arises.

Repetition, emotion and memory

By now you probably realise that people have many negative automatic responses to situations they encounter in the world. How can we help people choose new positive ways of responding in the world? The answer is that we need to be able to go from thinking to doing to being different. So how can we help our children change their behaviour? It begins with their thinking and this involves creating new knowledge in order to give them new choices.

In the example above, with my help, my child expanded her view of the world and gained new knowledge about how she could behave in the world if a similar situation arose in relation to sharing a toy. While this knowledge is good, it is still only knowledge and remains in the realm of thinking. The next step is to help her make the transition from thinking to doing. This involves helping my child remember the new knowledge she has learned and to be able to actually behave differently based on that new knowledge. That is, I need to help her move from thinking new thoughts to doing new behaviours. In this way the ideas become more than just ideas, they become life experiences.

The end product of positive new experiences is that they give rise to positive emotions and to more knowledge about how good this new way of behaving is. Then, to help your child move from doing to being is simply a matter of practice. The more times your child actually practises sharing, the more enjoyment they get from this experience, the more it becomes automatic in their nature so it becomes who they are in the world – it is who they are being. Once your child has shared many times, they become so practised at it, that they are just good at sharing and it comes naturally because they have done it many times and it brings about so much enjoyment.

So the next step in the process is to ask my child to repeat the ideas we have just shared on a new way to act if a situation arises where she needs to share. In this way I can check her understanding and help her if she has any misunderstandings or gaps in her knowledge about what to do in a new situation that calls for her to share. Asking your child to explain what they have learned also strengthens their ability to recall the information. When you were a child, you might remember repeating your times tables over and over again until you could remember them by heart. It is the same thing here.

In addition to working with her conscious mind through repetition, I want to work with her unconscious mind, in order to increase the likelihood that she will behave in a new way when confronted with the same situation. So I ask my child to close her eyes and I talk her through imagining herself experiencing a new way of being in the world. I talk her though the situation so she can see herself doing exactly what it was we said she would do when she experienced a situation where she needed to share a toy. I would talk her though how happy she now feels, how easy it is to share, how good it feels to be playing happily with her brother, how good they both feel, and how relieved she feels that she didn't end up in a fight with her brother by not sharing. For example, the text could be something like this:

> Dad: Now close your eyes and use your imagination. See yourself playing with your brother and notice that you are both going for the same toy. Hear yourself talking over how you are going to play together. Notice how happy you feel about negotiating how to play with the toy, notice how you want to make sure both you and your brother have a turn and that you both feel happy. See yourself getting the timer and agreeing to have 10 minutes each. See how you toss a coin to see who goes first, see how you pass the toy over once the ten minutes is over. Remember how nice it is to share, how good it feels to play together, how valuable it is to have this life skill to be able to share things with others. Remember that, know that you are a good sharer because that is who you are …

Notice how I have asked my child to use many of her senses in the dialogue. I asked her to see herself (visual), hear herself (auditory), feel how good it feels (emotions) … the more senses you can bring in to the visualisation exercise the more likely your child will subsequently remember and act in a new way when they need to share a toy.

The processes of asking your child to open their eyes and explain out loud to you what they will do when the next opportunity arises where they can choose to share and then subsequently asking them to close their eyes and imagine how they will share as you narrate the future experience for them is then repeated a number of times. It is repeated as many times as your child will allow and your mind will allow … repeat it while it is still fun! Make it fun … maybe speed it up … maybe slow it down … maybe say 'Hey, I'm not sure how it goes can you tell me again … ha … ha …' The important thing is that your children repeat the new knowledge many times in different forms so that they are more likely to act differently when the situation arises. Without going into too much detail about how this process happens in the brain, it is helpful to know that repetition creates and reinforces the new pathways (circuits) in the brain so that when the same situation comes up again your child will have the new knowledge in their brain circuits in place for dealing with it in the new way you practised together rather than the old way. You are helping to condition your child's body to respond in the new way ahead of the experience so they are ready when the experience arises. If the circuits in the brain are used they strengthen – just like muscles strengthen with repetition and the reverse is also true, muscles or brain circuits weaken if not used. Put very simply, the more children practise their times tables with different problems, the stronger their brain circuits become and the more they will be able to recognise when to use their times tables and be able to recall the right response. It is very helpful to explain why the repetition is beneficial to your child to help them understand and be more willing to participate in the process. Remember, the more fun you make it the more likely they will play along! So be creative!

Then I would end the bedtime emotional intelligence learning experience by telling a magical story that describes the same situation I was exploring with my child but using wonderful characters who 'resemble' my children. In the story I talk about two children and I describe them with the same physical characteristics as my children and how they were fighting over some magical thing and how bad they felt … and then one child came up with a great idea of getting a magical talking alarm clock to measure the time for them and they tossed a gold coin from a pirates' chest to see who will go first and then see themselves sharing and how happy they are and how good it feels and how much they love playing together, etc. As you can see this part of the exercise allows you to get your imagination going and inspire your children's interest! Make it magical and fun!

Once the story is over I wait. Many times one of my children will say 'was that story about us dad?' and I'll say 'do you think it was about you?' and when they say 'yes' … I kiss them good night and leave them to sleep so that they integrate their learning.

As my children got older they outgrew my fairy, pirate and superhero stories. However, we would talk over our day and go through similar collaborative learning processes every night. This allowed me to continue to help them to learn more and more sophisticated ways to operate in the world as they became ready for it. Year by year they came to understand more and more about how important it was for them to be able to recognise their emotions and be sensitive to the emotions of others which enabled them to communicate in life-enhancing and cooperative ways. As my children matured I would replace the magical fairy stories with myths, legends or other more age-appropriate stories that I had heard which would suit the emotional dilemma or personal experiences we were looking at.

For example, a powerful story which highlights the importance of developing emotional intelligence is one about a son who asked his father for advice on the eve of his wedding. The son asked the father what should I do to have a happy married life with my new wife? The father asked his son to come outside and he sat with his son on the back porch of his house overlooking his garden which was surrounded by a long, brown, wooden fence. His father said:

> I don't have all the answers to living a happy life, you must find those together with your wife, but I believe this advice will help you achieve your goal. Every time you get angry, upset or disappointed with your wife I want you to say nothing, go to your tool box, get a hammer and some nails and then hammer as many nails as you need to into this fence until you feel calm and ready to talk things over with your wife with care.

The son didn't really understand this, but as a respectful son he diligently did as his father suggested. After one year, the son had a lovely marriage, was very happy but now the fence was filled with nails, there was no more room and the thousands of nails had made the fence so heavy it was almost falling over. So the son called the father to find out what he should do next. They sat in the backyard and talked. The son asked the father what he should do to keep his marriage happy now that there was no more room in the fence for nails.

The father said:

> Every time you get angry, upset or disappointed with your wife I want you to say nothing, go to the tool box get a nail remover and remove

as many nails as you need to from this fence until you feel calm and ready to talk things through with your wife with care.

Again the son didn't really understand this, but as a respectful son he diligently did as his father suggested. After one more year, the son still had a lovely marriage, and was very happy but the fence was empty of nails and filled with holes and so the son called his father to find out what he should do next. The father and son sat in the backyard and talked. The son asked the father what he should do now that there were no more nails in the fence to remove. The father asked the son to describe what he saw. The son saw a fence nearly falling down with lots of holes in it. The father in his wisdom explained:

> Son, had you expressed your anger with your wife every time you were upset with her it would have been like putting a nail into her as you did in the fence. And even if you try and remove the nail with a sorry, it still leaves a hole. As you can see the fence is ruined as may have been your marriage.

The son realised how important it was to have emotional intelligence to lead a happy life. This little story can be adapted to suit your child's circumstances and development. For example, instead of a husband and wife the story could be between two best friends.

I'll conclude this chapter with a summary of the ways I helped my children develop emotional intelligence. I:

- Played games with them to practise feeling different emotions, which is emotional rehearsal.
- Observed my children when they were emotional so they could become aware of their own emotions and develop their conscious awareness. This helped my children separate themselves from their emotions.
- Explained how both negative and positive emotional predispositions develop starting with a mood, continuing into a temperament and ending in an emotional predisposition or personality trait. Therefore in order to change our personality we need to change the emotions we have memorised.

- Had my children engage in the catch your emotions game throughout their day.
- Helped my children develop new knowledge about how to manage their emotions, have empathy for others and create better social relationships.
- Helped my children remember the new knowledge through repetition visualisation and mental rehearsal techniques. I often refer to this as installing the 'hardware' of the brain ahead of the actual life experience, my children can now modify their behaviour and produce a different outcome when the experience arises.
- Talked about the importance of moving from thinking to doing to being.

These processes helped my children gain new knowledge, then act on that new knowledge and then practise and experience a new way of being with emotional intelligence.

Further readings

Beck AT (1976). *Cognitive therapy and the emotional disorders.* New York: International Universities Press.

Dispenza J (2007). *Evolve your brain: the science of changing your mind.* Deerfield Beach, Florida: Health Communications Inc.

Goleman D (1995). *Emotional intelligence: why it can matter more than IQ.* London: Bloomsbury Publishing Plc.

Salovey P & Mayer JD (1990). Emotional intelligence. *Imagination, Cognition and Personality*, 9: 185–211.

6

Parenting psychologically healthy children

L. Michael Hall, PhD

Caring for the physical wellbeing and safety of your children is a difficult part of parenting, but even more challenging is taking care of their psychological wellbeing. Let's face it, the physical is so much easier simply because it's tangible and you can see and hear if they are not well. It's the intangibility and the invisibility of a child's inner world that makes taking care of their psychological wellbeing more difficult.

- After all, what do you look at and notice to determine if a child's 'sense of self' is healthy and robust?
- What can you examine to check on your child's ego-strength, self-esteem and social-self?

Research on the psychology of 'self' and how it develops, helps us answer these crucial parenting questions. Our 'sense of self' is comprised of numerous factors. It is made up of self-esteem, self-confidence, ego, ego-strength, locus of control and social self among others. Perhaps it seems as though you'd need a degree in psychology to unravel and understand all of these 'selves'. However, as a parent, you can effectively respond to the challenge of supporting the psychological wellbeing of your children without having to get a degree in psychology. The first step is to distinguish self-esteem from self-confidence. This is one of, if not the most important steps in parenting psychologically healthy children.

Self-esteem and self-confidence

Self-esteem and self-confidence are often used interchangeably even though they are entirely different aspects of the self. So what's the difference? Self-esteem refers to a person's innate value, worth, dignity, honour, and lovability. It has nothing to do with what people can do, what they are good at or their talents, dispositions, gifts, or achievements. Those facets define self-confidence.

As a verb, esteem refers to a mental evaluation or judgment. It refers to how you appraise the value of something, and so it is based on a criterion or several criteria. But what criterion? When it comes to self-esteem, upon what can you base your evaluation? Is that evaluation conditional or unconditional? If conditional, then upon what conditions? Do you base the evaluation on a person's looks, intelligence, skills, cooperative nature, strength, speed, grades, money, relationships or some other factor? Whatever you base the person's value on – that then becomes the self-esteem conditions that you use – consciously or unconsciously to make the evaluation or judgment.

When valuing a person as having value, esteem, worth, dignity or honour, if it's conditional, then the person has to earn it. The person has to prove him or herself worthy of the value we attribute. It follows then, that the person has to continually earn it and this puts them on a treadmill – always trying to prove him or herself. Conditional self-esteem means you are not okay in, and of, yourself and that you have to earn your right to be valued as a person. Now imagine doing that to our children! If as parents, our children feel that they have to earn the right to be valued then we rob them of their innate right to be valuable human beings irrespective of what they do or don't do. It makes sense that children who constantly feel the need to prove themselves to feel lovable and valuable will feel anxious about their lives.

By contrast, unconditional self-esteem makes the criterion singular – if you are a human being, you have innate worth and value. Your dignity and honour is a given, you were born with value and dignity. You don't have to prove anything to be seen, recognised, and accepted as a full human being. Then, if your worth is a given, you don't have to prove anything to be a somebody. You already are a somebody and now you have the right and freedom to fully express your 'somebodyness'. Now by contrast, imagine supporting that in our children! If as parents, our children feel that they are loved and valued then we support and nurture their innate right to be valuable human beings irrespective of what they do or don't do. It makes sense that children who feel lovable and valuable will feel good about their lives. To make it simple, I've summarised the main differences between the two below.

Self-esteem	
Conditional	Unconditional
Based on conditions	Based on no conditions
Earned	Recognised as a gift
Always 'on the line'	Never in question
Hoping to become a somebody	Born a somebody

Typically people confuse self-esteem and self-confidence and speak about these two states as if they are synonyms. They are not. Perhaps you do too, it's not surprising as even some psychology books still interchange these words and make no distinction between them. They present self-esteem as if it is something conditioned upon a person's feelings of confidence about achievements. Once that assumption is made, then it seems like common sense to encourage 'building up self-esteem' by encouraging a person to find his or her strengths and developing them. However, based on the explanation so far, if parents make self-esteem conditional then their children have to 'earn' their worth, they are not valued in their own right.

A sign of this confusion shows up in our language every time we speak about high or low self-esteem. Yet, if self-esteem can be high (or low), then it is conditional. If it can go up or down then it's conditional and means it can even be lost. By contrast, if your esteem as a human being is unconditional, then your worth or value is unquestionable. You simply attribute to yourself, and everyone else, the honour and dignity of being a human being and therefore special, unique, valuable and sacred. In this case, self-esteem cannot go up or down or be lost. It simply is now and always!

The how of self-esteeming

Since this is not how most people think about self-esteem, the question arises: How do we give self-esteem to our children? How do we distinguish their worth and humanness from their activities and achievements?

When I became a parent, and especially a single-parent raising a daughter from the age of three years old by myself, I was especially aware to make this distinction. It was actually quite an easy thing to do – supported mostly by my words and the language I used. What I found challenging was to remember this as she grew up and became a teenager! Here are some of the things I would say to help her distinguish between the doing (conditional) and the being (unconditional):

- You did that really well! I think that's one of your strengths (or gifts). Well done.
- Whether you succeed in the meet/exam/game today or not, you are an absolutely valuable and lovable person and nothing can take away from you. So go out there, give it your best; have fun and we'll see what happens.
- Well, I think you know what I'm going to say. Don't you? Yes, you shouldn't have done that. And you know what the consequences are – you have to do a time-out in your bedroom. BUT, before you go I want you to know that I love you absolutely!

Ultimately, the answer is that it's not all that difficult or complex to support your child's self-esteem if you know the self-esteem/self-confidence difference and apply in your day-to-day parenting. To do that, think about something that you esteem or judge as having innate worth and value. Do you have anything like that? Have you ever stood in amazement at something, or in awe of something that just is, and that doesn't have to do anything to be so recognised? Here are some scenarios you may have experienced:

- Holding a newborn baby in your arms and feeling a sense of awe in the beauty of the child, the mystery of life, the magic of love, the wonder of the baby's humanity?

- Standing in awe of a beautiful sunrise or sunset, recognising the wonder of the planet circling the sun and spinning around.

- Standing on top of a mountain on a cloudless night and seeing the Milky Way Galaxy and sensing the immensity of the universe.

The feeling of awe results when you recognise the ultimate sense of esteem, worth, or value. So when you feel awe, take a moment to capture that feeling, to be with that feeling. That's the feeling of accepting or acknowledging the value and worth of something for what it is. Now, taking that feeling, apply that to yourself and acknowledge that being a human being is something that just is. Now stand in awe of that mystery, that awesome sacredness of what you are.

Doing that is self-esteeming, and being a good model of this, is critical for your child. Next, do it with your child. Take that feeling of awe and apply it to your child so that you can stand in awe of your child's innate worth and value and as you do, recognise that it is unconditional. Say to yourself, 'My child doesn't have to prove anything or achieve anything to be fully valuable as a person'. Now say this to your child. Declare this as a fact that you simply recognise – your child is a somebody. He or she doesn't have to prove anything, or earn anything. Your child already is an awesome being with incredible possibilities.

Then, invite your children to self-esteem in the same way you did. Help them to feel as much as possible the awe, love or happiness in something. Then invite them to take that feeling and apply it to themselves and acknowledge that being a human being is something that just is. Invite them to say 'I am special and lovable as I am and I don't have to do anything or be anything to be loved'. Children have a wonderful imagination and capacity to feel and the more they practise self-esteeming the better they will get at loving and valuing themselves for who they are![1]

---

1 In the appendix I have provided an exercise you can use yourself or with your child to help them with acceptance, appreciation and awe.

Appreciate your child's powers and achievements

If self-esteem is about your value as a being, then self-confidence is about your faith in yourself in relation to doing. The word 'confidence' tells the story. *Fideo* is faith or trust which you have 'with' (con) yourself. In other words, it's about your trust or belief in your ability to do something. What are you confident about? Typing? Riding a bike? Washing your clothes? Cooking a meal? Reading? Whatever it is, you are confident about your skill or ability to do something. In contrast, if you have a skill that you are just learning, you're probably not confident about it – yet. But, if you keep at it, keep learning, experimenting, practising, and receiving feedback then you will develop the feeling of confidence in relation to that skill.

Unlike self-esteem, self-confidence is conditional. You have to earn it. You have to prove that you can actually do the thing that you're confident about. So when parenting, you can support your child's development of self-confidence by: finding what they can do; helping them learn new information, support them in developing the skill, and in celebrating the achievement.

But there is one important caution here. Don't make the child's sense of self-value conditional upon his or her skills, gifts, strengths, or successes. Yes, value them, appreciate them, and esteem the child's skills and achievements, but don't connect them to making the child a better person or somehow more valuable. It does not. Sure, the child's accomplishments will influence his or her self-confidence, and it should. But don't link this to his or her value as a human being. It does not make the child one iota of a more valuable person just because they can do something.

The way to do this is to watch how you praise. Here is a supportive example where you encourage the talent but don't link it to the value of the child.

> You are really good at music (or whatever). You have an ear for it! That's good, maybe you would like to learn to play an instrument or join the choir.

The other side of this is enabling your child to accept and to live comfortably with the areas in which he or she is not naturally talented and still feel innately valuable:

> You're really good at mathematics and so your gifts make you different from your brother who's really good at music. It's okay. Now you can focus your interest on your talent and potentials just like he can. Isn't that great?

The person who demands the feeling of confidence in something prior to learning is requiring the impossible or the unrealistic. I say 'the impossible' because to have confidence in yourself that you can do something before you do it is by definition – impossible. And I say unrealistic because if you did access a feeling of confidence regarding something that in reality you are incompetent in – then that feeling of confidence would be unrealistic. You would feel that you could do something when you cannot! As you can imagine, this could lead to all sorts of strife!

Before I move on to introducing the concept of self-efficacy, the differences between self-confidence and self-esteem are summarised below for easy reference.

Self-esteem	Self-confidence
Human being - about being-ness	Human doing - about talents and skills
Being as a person	Doing as an achiever
Unconditional	Conditional
Don't have to prove yourself	Must prove yourself
Realm of 'person'	Realm of competency and achieve-ment
Be in order to do	Do in order to do
Your value as a person	Faith or trust in what you can do

The diagram below helps you see that as parents we would like our child's self-esteem to always be at 100% throughout their entire life. Whereas, we would like our child's self-confidence to grow as they experience and learn in the world.

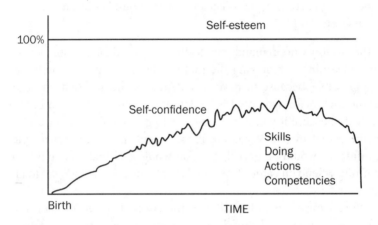

Moving from self-confidence to self-efficacy

Once children develop confidence in one thing, and then another, and then many others, eventually when they become teenagers another state can emerge. When you develop self-confidence once and again in a variety of areas, it means that you have repeatedly moved from incompetence to competence. It means you have learned and developed one particular skill, and then another. At first, each new skill or aptitude always seems so hard and so impossible. But eventually, you realise that it's just the learning process. It is with that realisation and that understanding that self-efficacy begins.

What's the difference? Self-confidence relates to the past and to the skills that you have already developed. Your confidence in what you can do has proof and evidence to back it up. You know you can do something because you have done it before and you have done it often enough that you now trust yourself, and now feel convinced that you can do it again and again. Self-efficacy relates to the future and to the skills that you will develop, or even could develop if you so choose. Your sense of confidence in those yet-to-be-developed skills of the future has no historical proof, no evidence that you can point to and say, 'see I have done that before!' Instead what convinces you of self-efficacy is something else, it's your sense of confidence in you, in your ability to learn, to develop, to go through the learning process. It's your sense of confidence that you can trust your wits, your intelligence, your emotions, your ability to relate to others, and so on. That's self-efficacy.

As an example, I have a sense of self-confidence in driving a car. I've been driving since I was 16 and have driven without an accident of any sort for over 30 years. Further, I have driven in countries that drive on the right side of the road (in the US) and the left side (in Australia). I have lots of history that can boost up my confidence about driving a car. But since I have never flown a plane, I do not have confidence about doing that. But I have a sense of self-efficacy that I could fly a plane in the near future if I so chose. Why? How? Because I know that it's just a matter of learning and practice. I know that I could sign up for a course or get a private tutor to guide me through the process. I know of many friends who have their pilot's license and I could speak with them about the process.

It is also self-efficacy, rather than self-confidence, that gives a child a sense of taking on the world and following his or her dreams and isn't that what we all want for our children? With the right conditions and support, our children can eventually learn that the early stages of not knowing something and feeling incompetent in a new area, and sometimes even overwhelmed, is just part of the process of becoming competent. There's no need to misread or overload that experience with negative meanings. It is the process everybody goes through in developing competence and then mastery. The difference between self-esteem and self-confidence are summarised on the following page for easy reference.

Self-confidence	Self-efficacy
Able to do something/development of a skill	Not able to do something yet
Able to achieve an activity or experience	Faith or trust in self that you will be able to develop a new skill or competence
From incompetence to competence and then to expertise	Realisation that having developed many competencies in the past means can trust one's future ability to learn
Proof from the past	Abilities and potentials

Enable your child to develop a strong ego

'Ego' is simply a Greek word for 'self', 'I' or 'me'. There's nothing wrong with 'ego' or having an ego though it has been known to have negative connotations in everyday use. Every thinking person who faces reality has an 'ego'. For Sigmund Freud, ego refers to 'the reality principle' and so to our ability to face reality for what it is.

As a sense of self, no one is born with an 'ego'. At first, a newborn infant is undifferentiated from mother. Then ever so slowly, the infant begins to discover itself to be a self, one separate from mother. And this differentiation and individuation continues until the young child knows him or herself as a separate person. So ego-strength is the strength of your sense of self to look at what is in the face without falling apart, caving in, or having some fight or flight response. No one is born with this, it develops. It develops as we develop a sense of our value and our confidence in our skills. It especially develops as we develop effective skills in coping with our basic needs and drives.

It is appropriate to expect that your children will not have ego-strength for many years. It comes over time as part of their mental, emotional and behavioural development. It develops as they learn to use their mind and actions to cope effectively with the challenges in their lives and as they learn to use their intellect to figure things out. Parents can support the natural development of ego-strength in their children by asking them questions that are appropriate to their age and maturity. The aim is to ask questions that invite them to use their brains to 'figure things out' for themselves. Discovering that they can work things out, that they can influence things, that they are not helpless, but that there's rhyme and reason to life, gives them confidence in their abilities and social skills.

Ego-strength is a consequence of discovering and developing your four innate powers – your mental powers, emotional powers, verbal (or linguistic) powers, and powers of action. These four powers enable you to feel in control of yourself – your mind, emotions, and verbal and behavioural responses. This creates a sense of empowerment and a response-ability. Parents can help their children to develop a sense of response-ability bringing your children's awareness to their thoughts, their emotions and their actions. Questions like 'What do you think about that?' 'How do you feel?', 'What would you do in this situation?' Then you can help your children make links by relating their thinking and their feelings. 'If that's what you think, doesn't it make sense that you are feeling X?' For example 'If you think that you can't speak in front of people, doesn't it make sense that you feel really nervous about tomorrow?'

You may have noticed that the sense of 'ownership' emerges very early in children, somewhere in the second year. That's when they first learn the word, 'mine'. This isn't a sign of selfishness, but of the development of personality and the beginnings of taking ownership and responsibility. As children welcome things, experiences, and people into their world, they become richer within themselves. When parents think about it that way, it opens up new possibilities for nurturing their development. If parents don't criticise or demonise this natural part of a child's personal growth, they can support the development of a sense of ownership for his or her thoughts, emotions, words, and actions – the key variables for responsibility and proactivity.

As a single parent I was acutely aware that my daughter's sense of self, was in my hands and that it was a huge responsibility and fragile gift. My interactions and experiences with her showed me that her sense of self could easily be hurt, wounded, distorted, or even devastated because she was a child and not a little adult.

Children, even into their teenage years, are fluid and malleable and in the process of becoming who they will become. They can so easily misinterpret things parents and others close to them can say or do and create distortions in their personalities. I believe our task as parents is to provide guidance that allows age-appropriate freedom within a context of love. And yet this love needs to be firm, without being over-controlling, and yet gracious and understanding. Such is the dance of parenting! Your children will develop a solid, robust, and resilient sense of themselves in an environment that allows for self-discovery and the space to be able to use personal powers to face the challenges of life in a resilient way.

It all begins with helping your child understand the difference between self-esteem and self-confidence, and supporting the development in time of self-efficacy and a strong sense of self. In this way we give our children the best chance to lead a happy and inspired life!

Appendix 1

I'd like to share one of the activities I use myself and I have used with my daughter many times as she was growing up to help her experience self-acceptance, self-appreciation and self-esteem.

Supporting your 'self' activity

The following activity is the process for inducing three basic self states: self-acceptance, self-appreciation and self-esteem.[2] You can use it to establish a solid core for centering yourself and your children, for setting a positive mindset of high value and worth for oneself, and for operating with high self-esteem even in the face of life experiences that may be dignity-denying or threatening. I have used three states of being (acceptance, appreciation and awe). In this example, the continuum is to do with liking and welcoming something into your world but you can use the same activity for other things.

The key distinctions you will be making as you use this activity are the distinctions between self-esteem as unconditional (based on an

---

2 For more about the meta-states model and the process of meta-stating, see Hall 2001, 2007 and 2009.

evaluation or judgment of the mind) and self-confidence as conditional (based on competency and experience). For the best results for this activity ask these questions: Do you ever judge yourself as a human being? Do you ever put yourself down? Contempt yourself? Insult yourself? Do you have low self-esteem? Do you separate your feelings about you as a human being from your feelings as a human doing? Then let's try this activity to allow you to experience acceptance, appreciation and awe for yourself instead! A much more powerful state to be in.

The activity

1) Feel each of the three states of being – acceptance, appreciation, and awe.

You can feel or access each state by using a small and simple referent so that you can access the feeling of the state fully and discreetly.

A) Acceptance

What do you accept that you could reject? What small and simple thing do you easily accept without particularly liking or wanting, but you welcome? Once you may have hated it, rejected it, got yourself upset about it, but now you find that things go better by just accepting it. A menu list for *acceptance* includes asking questions like can you accept when it's raining, the traffic, taking out the garbage, putting up with noise at the coffee shop, or for a child eating food every day, going to the toilet, maybe brushing one's teeth, etc.

(Acceptance is not resignation nor is it condoning. It is acknowledging what *is* as that which exists and has to be dealt with for what it is. Acceptance is typically a very small and gentle feeling in the body. Notice your breath, posture, face, eyes, etc. when you are in that state.)

B) Appreciation

Is there anything that you really appreciate? What do you really value and appreciate that causes you to melt in appreciation? A menu list: holding a newborn baby, watching a beautiful sunset, having a glass of wine with a friend, a back rub, walking on a beach with a loved one, or for a child eating ice-cream and playing with puppies, etc.

(Appreciation goes far beyond acceptance as it warmly welcomes the valued object. Appreciation is the most emotional of these three states and most easily experienced in the body.)

C) Awe

What is so big, so wonderful, so marvelous, so incredible that you stand in awe of it, speechless, in utter wonder? Menu list: standing in the presence of one of the 'Wonders of the World,' being present at the birth of your child, seeing the Milky Way Galaxy on the top of a mountain, contemplating your understanding of the spiritual, or for a child seeing their favourite cartoon character in real life, experiencing a ride at an amusement park etc.

(Awe, by its very nature, is much less emotional and sometimes involves the feeling of being speechless, beyond words, a state in which you may hold your breath and hardly move.)

2) Amplify each state of being and apply to yourself (or to the child you are working with)

As you feel X (acceptance, appreciation, awe), how strong is that feeling? (From 0 to 10.) Now let that feeling grow, let it become stronger and stronger. Double the intensity of that feeling. Let it permeate throughout your body and radiate out. Do you now have a good robust state of X? Anchor[3] the state with a gesture and/or a touch, that is, link or associate a gesture or a touch to the experience of that state so that it becomes associated with the state.

---

3 'Anchoring' is a process in neurolinguistic programming (NLP) for linking or associating one thing with another. As such, it is a user-friendly version of conditioning in behaviourism. The process is described in most introduction books to NLP or you can find it in Hall & Belnap 2004 or Bodenhamer & Hall 2001.

Now one state of being at a time, apply the resource to yourself:

Apply acceptance to the things about yourself that you need to accept, but may find challenging to accept – your shadow side, experiences that have happened to you, the cards that life dealt you. Accept your overall sense of self and life.

What do you want to accept?

As you think about that, feel this (fire the trigger for acceptance).

Apply appreciation to your sense of self as doer and achiever. Appreciate your overall self, and every gift, talent, and strength. Feel this sense of appreciation to your mind, your emotions, your speech, your behaviour. (This separates self-confidence and self-esteem.)

What can you appreciate? What else?

As you feel this, notice what else you can appreciate.

Apply awe and esteem to your self as a valuable, precious, magnificent human being unconditionally. (Use self-esteem to enrich self-appreciation and self-acceptance.)

Feeling this self-esteem fully and completely, letting it grow and expand ... that's right, now notice what else you can *appreciate* (fire anchor) and what else you can just *accept* (fire anchor) more gracefully and easily. That's right.

3) Apply self-esteeming, appreciating, and accepting to different contexts in your life

Is there any context, situation, or event wherein you feel tempted to self-contempt, self-question, self-doubt, and/or self-dislike yourself?

In what context do you want to operate from with a solid sense of your unconditional self-esteem?

As you think about that, *feel this esteem* (fire anchor) for yourself knowing that your worth and value is a given and *feel this appreciation* for what you can do so that you focus there, and *feel this acceptance* of the things that just are and that you have to deal with.

Now especially notice how *feeling this esteem and self-awe* at the mystery of you and your potentials transforms this old context. How is that?

Do you like that? Would that make a difference?

Are you ready to self-respect yourself no matter what?

Are you ready to step into unconditional self-esteem?

4) Imaginatively put into your future to validate

Imagine moving through life in the weeks and months to come with this frame of mind of self-acceptance, self-appreciation, and self-esteem … Do you like this?

Notice how this would transform things for you …

Does every aspect of the higher parts of your mind fully agree with this?

Is your sense of your own value now completely set?

Further readings

Bodenhamer BG & Hall LM (2001). *The user's manual for the brain. Volume 1.* Bancyfelin, Carmarthen, Wales: Crown House Publishing.

Hall LM (2009). *Meta-states: mastering the high levels of your mind.* 3rd edn. Bancyfelin, Carmarthen, Wales: Crown House Publishing.

Hall LM (2007). *Winning the inner game: mastering the inner game for peak performance.* Clifton, CO: Neuro-Semantic Publications.

Hall LM (2001). *Secrets of personal mastery: awakening your inner executive.* Bancyfelin, Carmarthen, Wales: Crown House Publishing.

Hall LM & Belnap BP (2004). *Sourcebook of magic: a comprehensive guide to NLP change patterns.* 2nd edn. Bancyfelin, Carmarthen, Wales: Crown House Publishing.

7

Helping children to manage stress

Maggie Dent

Today, more than ever before, our children are struggling in a chaotic, fast-paced, violent, uncertain and threatening world. It's pretty scary for us adults let alone our children. It can be argued that many adults aren't able to manage their stress because no-one helped them with stress and distress in their childhood so they haven't developed self-regulating systems in their brains (Sunderland 2007). Given we know that over 75% of illnesses are stress related and that the research on epigenetics discussed in chapter two of this book explains how distress from abusive or difficult childhoods can be passed on to future generations, it is crucial that parents, carers and educators equip our children with the tools they need to calm themselves, self-regulate and navigate safely in our chaotic world. In Australia 20 years ago around 5–10% of children had some form of significant developmental delay. That figure is now around 24%.

As a mother of four boys, a school teacher, and a parenting and resilience specialist, I have seen bullying, obesity, substance abuse, self-harm, suicide rates, and depression and other mental illnesses continue to increase among children. Our modern world has many toxic influences that impact on the wellbeing of our children. For many years I have explored and shared the ways we can support our children who are lost, troubled and disconnected from life. I've found that the key elements to creating happy and healthy kids lie in helping children find stillness, calm, connectedness and a sense that they matter.

As a child I experienced emotional deprivation, deep criticism and physical abuse from my alcoholic mother. I used to escape Mum by spending time in nature in the bush, in the paddocks or in our orchard where I played imaginative games or simply sat and felt free. It took years to realise the physical abuse did less damage than the absence of love, kindness and positive touch. My teen years were pretty miserable even though I was able to achieve academically and in sport. I was largely disconnected from others to avoid being hurt, and yet I could fake that I was a friend. My vulnerable, wounded parts were totally hidden and the mask I wore fooled everyone.

After my failed suicide attempt at 17, I decided I wanted to help teenagers grow through this confusing stage of life better than I had. Later as a high school English teacher I began to explore solutions for troubled children simply by treating them with more kindness, empathy and concern. I knew that feeling invisible, voiceless and that no-one cares were common messages from troubled teenagers. In my resilience studies I have discovered that one of the most significant protective factors we can have in life is positive human connectedness and a notion that we belong.

I was once stopped by a hairy black-leathered biker who asked if I remembered him? Many years before he had been a very quiet little boy in a Year 8 class. He wanted to tell me how important it had been for him to be able to come to my classes often without his file or biros to know that I always kept spare ones in case he forgot to bring them. It was the only class where he could feel safe not to be ridiculed or shouted at. He then told me why he often came without his things: both parents were alcoholics and sometimes it was not safe to go home. His grandmother would often care for him and if she was also drunk or away he would sleep in the park. He thanked me and told me he had learned what kindness was from me. I wish I had known more at the time – such is the power of that mask that teens can wear.

Children and families in crisis

This example is not unique, as much as I wish it were. Today's world is full of so many innovations, new knowledge and new ways of doing things, we should all be in great shape! Unfortunately we are not. The many phone calls and emails I get from parents and teachers who are deeply concerned about young children and teenagers, and how they are managing and coping with the pressures of modern living, show a new level of concern.

Many parents strive to be 'perfect' while living incredibly busy, ever-changing lives. Their own exhaustion and stress only adds to children's stress and creates an invisible pressure on families. Calmness and quiet has become difficult to factor into our schedules and yet we know that calm adults:

- are less clumsy or accident prone
- use a softer voice
- are less forgetful
- are more organised
- are more patient
- sleep better.

As adults struggle, research also supports the perception of the declining health and wellbeing of our young. Of most concern is the increasing numbers of children and adolescents who are succumbing to depression, emotional instability, mental illnesses, obesity and low educational and social competence. We are seeing:

- more violence and assaults
- more children on attention deficit hyperactivity disorder (ADHD) medication to manage hyperactivity and inability to concentrate
- more children presenting with depression or emotional overwhelm and overload
- more cases of sexual abuse
- more children suffering obesity and diabetes
- more children suffering alcohol and drug abuse
- more children homeless
- more children being diagnosed with obsessive compulsive disorder and severe anxiety
- children as young as three on sleeping medication to help them sleep

- children under five on antidepressants
- an increase in childhood and juvenile crime
- no real improvement in school retention rates for our Indigenous children
- an ever increasing teen suicide rate.

Unfortunately this is not a new phenomenon. Professor Fiona Stanley, a world authority on child health, expressed her concerns at a conference almost a decade ago:

> Health and behaviour problems among children have reached frightening levels and a national campaign is needed to avert a looming social crisis. (*West Australian*, 9 November 2002)

While some issues are easy to see, many pressures and challenges are invisible. What can be helpful on one level can be destructive on another like TVs, mobile phones, the internet, tablets and mp3 players. Being affluent and having the ability to give your children things you were unable to have as a child should be a good thing. Unfortunately affluence can create more challenges to raising happy, balanced and resilient children than financial challenge or adversity.

My heart goes out to all parents and children experiencing hardship, and I keep questioning – why? Why so much anguish? Why are so many children in crisis? Why is this happening to our children and in such epidemic proportions?

Obviously, there is no simple answer to this question but there are contributing factors including the speed at which we live our lives.

The pace of life

Most people would agree the pace of life and living has sped up. This presents children with the huge challenge of living in a chaotic world and the need to develop strategies to avoid becoming overwhelmed by the busy-ness of life. The 'hurried child' and the 'over-scheduled' child are both modern developments. Somewhere in the last 10 years parenting has become a type of competition and the hidden stress this places on growing children causes many other issues that delay healthy development and growth on all levels emotionally, socially, spiritually and cognitively. The main sources of stress and anxiety in children include:

- hurried, overscheduled world
- temperaments and personality
- absence of healthy love and attachment
- too much pressure on children to perform
- stressed parents who rush
- not enough calm, still, quiet solo time
- poor sleep patterns
- too much stimulation from TV, toys and adult commands
- not enough consistency and routines
- too much social change
- shaming language and discipline techniques
- threats of abuse and violence
- the effects of increased use of social media (Twitter, Facebook, My Space, Youtube) on the growth of a child's identity and character
- dependence on electronic gadgets and technology (smart phones, games, iPods, computers) that steal attention, time and presence.

There has been a significant increase in the number of children suffering from anxiety and stress related illnesses and hyper-sensitive behaviours. Busy parents who have poor stress regulating systems often contribute to the increased levels of stress in their children. All this stress has long term consequences. Margot Sunderland (2007) argues that scientists link the stress experienced in infancy and childhood to the increasing numbers of people suffering from anxiety and depressive disorders from adolescence and into adulthood. The additional stress in children's lives shapes their capacity to self-regulate their energy and their emotions and this has been shown to have a huge influence on their capacity to learn and do well in the school environment.

We live in an instant world where we expect everything NOW. Communication, food, pain relief, results, well-behaved children – you name it, we expect it instantly. This expectation works silently and unconsciously creates stress when things do not always happen like that. Children take all of childhood to grow – to learn how to think, learn, process information, behave appropriately – manage their lives, dress themselves, find their way home and learn who they are. We cannot rush this vital development. We all need to slow down – simplify our lives and spend more time committed to being a positive part of our kids' lives.

Love, love, love

As an independent counsellor and educational consultant with a special interest in emotional literacy and human resilience I see the broken spirits and damaged minds from not raising children with love, awareness and healthy parenting practices. Our children's world can be made better. I know that because I am witnessing it in homes and schools where the emotional wellbeing of children does come first. Research has long shown that happy, calm children learn best. A safe environment where differences are accepted and respected allows children to learn social skills as well as academic skills. Humans are programmed to be social animals. Social behaviour is not inherent. It happens through the constant interaction of humans with other humans over a long period of time.

Children, now more than ever, require input into their learning and growth. Children respond to people who let them explore their own choices and give them the opportunity to make more of their own decisions within safe boundaries. Over-parenting and helicopter parenting diminish children's capacity to cope with change and adversity later. However, boundaries are important and sometimes the most loving thing to do for a child is to discipline them for inappropriate behaviour. We are not meant to be our children's best friend – we have to be their parent to teach and guide them how to be healthy, happy, strong and kind.

Making choices and finding meaning

Children need to find a reason for being here on this planet. This deep search for purpose seems to be present now in many children from an early age. Without discovering 'a reason for being' many of our wise teenagers become deeply disillusioned with our world and their own lives and become lost in depression and other forms of mental illness or hide in alcohol and drug abuse.

It's crucial to imbue a sense of hope in our young people and to strengthen their spirits by allowing some magic and imagination in life, encouraging them to spend time in nature and caring for the environment and practising acts of kindness. Kindness is so important to building our own spirit and sense of value and it's something we've always encouraged in our household by doing things like cooking for sick family or friends, looking after neighbours' houses and pets when they're away, or leaving notes of gratitude for each other.

The 'highs' of alcohol, drugs and ...

Where young people do feel hopeless, it's easy for them to turn to alcohol and drugs in their search for joy.

The sad fact is substance abuse has increased considerably over the last 10 years but what is behind this? Substances are easily accessed by young people, even in schools. Legal drugs, including tobacco, alcohol and pharmaceutical drugs have increased in use and social acceptance. Experts vary in their opinions and their reasons for increased abuse range from 'it is normal for teenagers to experiment with drugs and alcohol' to 'the use of substances is a way to escape unhappiness and loneliness'.

If you ask teenagers themselves they say things like 'it's a way to de-stress and relax' or 'a way to have a 'peak experience' – to feel great'. In this way, drugs particularly alcohol and cannabis have become the stress release of modern teenagers and often fill the huge sense of loneliness and disconnectedness that many teenagers tell me they feel.

Through working with many teenagers who use illicit drugs to escape the pressures of adolescence, the way was opened for me to consider the need to give our children and teenagers the opportunity to experience stillness, connectedness and moments of heightened pleasure and wellbeing without drugs of any kind. The desire for connection, joy and transcendence is at the core of every human on their journey to awareness and maturity. Parents and teachers can help children find this heightened sense of connectedness and being, and it begins with slowing everything down and continues with patience and understanding.

A little patience and understanding goes a long way

I encourage all parents and people who work with children to remember that children are children – they have immature emotional literacy, gaps in their social education, delays in their development, a developing unfinished brain, confusion about needs and wants, and all of them wish to be loved and valued exactly as they are, not how they could be. This is normal for children – and many of the concerns may stem from the pressures of living in our chaotic world. We all need to step back from judging and criticising how children grow and develop; even children with special needs are still children who need play, fun and laughter to help them enjoy life. There are no quick fixes to raising children to be decent human beings, however, if you are worried about a child – slow their life down, connect with them from where they are, play with them or simply be with them in nature. Take the stress away for just a short time, create opportunities for them to experience natural and sustaining 'highs' to motivate and inspire them into living a happy, healthy and meaningful life.

Sporting 'highs'

Anyone who plays sport knows that it has huge potential for inducing drug-free highs in both the player and the observer. While I am a 'seldom TV-watcher' even I have witnessed some of the magic moments in sporting history. Australians have an international reputation of being an outdoors, 'sporting-mad' nation. Why? One reason is that sport elevates players and observers into a sporting high – a pleasurable state we all enjoy. Most importantly this high can be experienced without alcohol and drugs. Just recently Cadel Evans excited Australians with his victory in the Tour de France and many of these excited Australians do not own a bicycle!

It is therefore important for children to engage in and enjoy physical activities including sport. Athletic pursuits can be used as a drug prevention tool so it is important for schools and communities to be as proactive and supportive in the development of sport and encouraging children to be outdoors.

Being in nature

I was a farmer's daughter, so I grew up fully experiencing and being in nature as a place of comfort and enlightenment. In encouraging the growth of a healthy relationship with nature – the 'outside world' is of great importance to families. Growing up on a farm meant I spent a great deal of time outdoors and helped to deliver lambs by the age of six. I recall how exciting it was to actually help bring a lamb into the world. The more children experience growing up in nature, the more they can be aware of the passing of seasons and of the cycle of birth, life and death. Birth is a very transcendent experience – a natural high.

Research shows the alienation of city life can contribute to addictive behaviour, depressive thoughts or a sense of disconnection from nature, people and things that matter. Richard Louv's *Last child in the woods* (2008) explores the new phenomenon called nature-deficit disorder and the impact this has on a child's development throughout life.

Children spend too many hours contained in the four walls of their home and classroom. While most schools have sporting programs, it is important to increase participation by all students to at least one major physical challenge as part of the school program. This can be achieved if outdoor activities are readily accessible, are inspiring and cater for varying interests and abilities.

Older children, especially teenage boys, need adventures with greater physical challenges. Adventures on the tall ship *Leeuwin* are a great example of physical challenge. This challenge is not only physically demanding but also provides opportunities for character building, as well as a positive way to experience drug-free highs. The teens become part of the team. They are set the challenge of being responsible for the safety of everyone on board the ship – this can certainly be character building. The physical challenges enable tests of personal courage such as scaling the masts. Obviously close supervision is provided and the supervising adults have the expertise and the passion to support teenagers to grow. For younger children – school camps can offer exciting and age-appropriate outdoor challenges. Unfortunately, the screen world and massive explosion of laptops and interactive smart boards in classrooms has diminished the two main protective forces of human connectedness and a respectful bondedness to the natural world.

As parents and carers we can support children's pursuits of a variety of outdoor activities. It can be as simple as taking them to a local park, a weekend outdoor sporting activity or simply going for short walks in the neighbourhood. My sons are all keen surfers. Over the last 10 years, all four of them have experienced some of their finest and most challenging moments in the ocean. There is something very special about the ocean and it can help children connect to their soul just by being part of it. We can encourage our children to find this connection with the ocean or the natural environment and to nurture it.

Teenagers are often looking for a high. Healthy challenges like rock climbing, abseiling or high-ropes courses provide a 'buzz' and a thrill that comes from physical mastery and is a drug-free way for teenagers to experience a feeling beyond the normal. This invites healthy risk-taking rather than dangerous drug and alcohol use to achieve the same kind of high. We all grow when we challenge our comfort zones, whether physical or emotional. For my boys, like many others, the ocean helps to satisfy their desire to seek thrills, and might I add it is also good for their souls.

Challenges and active outdoor pursuits are great for active and able children – but if your child is not so sporty or has a physical limitation, perhaps they can find their natural high by expressing themselves through music or art.

Music and art

For centuries, the arts have provided people with a source of wonder, awe and entertainment. Painters, sculptors, musicians and singers stir our hearts and lift our spirits to elevated heights. However, it's important to remember that it's NOT just the great talents that can do this. You can feel the same awe and wonder at the giftedness of children at a school concert as they act, dance and sing their parts. Parents and grandparents alike can experience a sense of pride, warmth in the heart and a tear in the eye when they see their children perform.

The children and teenagers taking part in concerts, school plays, Rock Eisteddfods and musicals experience a heightened feeling of 'being' which is another great example of how children can experience a drug/alcohol-free lift. Most schools have dedicated and talented teachers who support students to put on amazing shows. To succeed, there are many hours of preparation, rehearsal and working together as a group for a shared goal. This helps children learn so many valuable life skills and helps boost their confidence as well as experience the sheer exhilaration of performing in front of an audience.

Rachael Kessler (2000) talks of 'the urge for transcendence' that young people seek. She includes the following quote from Neville in her book:

> Adolescents of all ages need ecstatic experience to become adult, and if the culture will not provide it they will seek it in any case, often in ways which do them harm.

This urge can in some cases translate into car accidents, near-death experiences, or alcohol and drug abuse. Kessler explored the fascination with death in teenagers and identified that some suicides were the result of a 'quest for a life-affirming experience of transcendence' rather than due to despair and hopelessness as discussed above. This quest can be spurred on by songwriters and celebrities who have died, like Michael Hutchence or Amy Winehouse.

According to Kessler, transcendence can be experienced in a variety of ways including: reaching beyond ordinary life and consciousness and opening to the spirit; being immersed in a play, dance or creative process; experiencing 'flashes of intensity' against a 'dull background' of ordinary days; or even rising above, or beyond, human limits.

In addition to nurturing children's creative expression, we need to create the space for them to express and share their feelings and thoughts. In this way we can have honest communication and connect with them on a deep level.

Connectedness

At their core, all human beings seek connectedness and communion. Children are no exception. Honest sharing though open-hearted discussions, where everyone is included and respected, provides the potential for everyone to experience deep connectedness. I have experienced this many times with my children, in my classrooms and with my clients. Deep, honest respectful sharing can create a deep sense of belonging and of being valued.

Connectedness and the need to belong is a driving force in a child's life, which is why we hear so much about peer pressure. An alienated teenager with few friends is the most at risk of struggling in life. That's why it's so important for parents to take steps to help their children make and keep good friends where possible. I'd like to share a difficult decision we had to make as a family that is relevant here.

When my eldest son began Year 7, he had been placed in a class separate from his two good friends. This son's teachers thought he was popular and would fit in anywhere, but in fact these two friends were the ones that mattered most to him. He came home and announced to me that he was not going back to that school – he wasn't happy. I knew that this emotion wasn't just coming from the class placement issue. This son wasn't particularly comfortable in this strict, private school where he was regularly reprimanded for having his shirt untucked. I said to him that I was prepared to consider him moving schools but that he would have to accept that once he moved, I would not move him back. I asked him to reflect on it and go and sit quietly on his own, really listening to himself, to sleep on it. He did so and he said that he knew he should move schools. I knew then that it might be the right choice and he went on to find his place in a new school that was far more suited to him.

On the other hand, changing schools can be very traumatising for children. I have worked with so many men who have suffered enormous trauma from being sent to boarding school or from moving town, city or state without being heard or listened to. Boys are not as well equipped to create new friends as our chatty and more social girls. And all children can suffer from a deep sense of loss of their home, family and their 'place' in the world when they move. The tricky thing about being a resiliency expert is that when it came to my kids I have needed to *walk my talk* not just talk it! When my younger son and I were separated due to me moving away for work while he was in Year 10, I had to put a lot of effort into making sure we both coped. I rang often, I sent funny cards, and I baked and sent boxes of cookies or chocolates to show my son I cared and still loved him. Also, I was really honest about my own feelings and shared them with him. It's OK for Mums and Dads (especially important for Dads) to cry or bawl with your child, friends or family. Change affects us on all levels and we need to be real enough to own the emotional aspects. This helps our children follow our example and develops their emotional wellbeing and resilience.

Children love connection and if they don't get it they will do almost anything to get your attention. Have you noticed how often your children want to chat while you are getting dinner ready, on the phone or when bedtime looms? We need to be available to really listen without our adult heads, and with compassion and concern for a fellow traveller on this journey of life. To hear them as they explore their thoughts and feelings is one of the most loving things an adult can do for a teenager. It is about being validated and feeling worthy of being heard.

Dr Daniel Siegel in his book *Mindsight: change your brain and your life* believes that deep human connectedness does so much more:

> the presence of a caring, trusted other person who is attuned to our internal world is often the initial key to widening our windows of tolerance – people need to 'feel felt' by someone – because the neural networks around the heart and throughout the body are intimately interwoven with the resonance circuits of the brain …

We must remember children are here to live their lives and not our expectation of their lives. This requires patience, unconditional love and valuing that they need to find their own path in life. The parents who allow their teenagers to explore our chaotic world for a sense of 'purpose and meaning' that is uniquely their own, while loving them and appreciating them, are the parents who will always be a positive part of their teenagers' lives when they become adults.

Purpose and meaning in life

In my work with children I share with them the idea that everyone's purpose on earth is to make the world a better place in some way. Each of us has a unique mix of talents and abilities and it's up to us to find a way to use them to improve something about our world. I help them discover the small ways first so they can experience a sense of achieving this task with an intention and little effort.

Doing things for others whether helping grandparents, coaching junior sports, mentoring or volunteering is excellent. Children can improve the environment by picking up rubbish, doing tree plantings or animal rescue.

It also needs to be acknowledged that there are many wonderful educators who are showing children how to take responsibility for their carbon footprint – there are vegie patches, worm farms, water tanks and solar panels popping up in child care centres and schools around Australia. It's a small but important step.

Another simple way to make the world better is to be a good friend through thick and thin. By starting simply, children can create that deep sense of having a value and reason for being here now instead of frightening themselves with the future. We can help them connect with their purpose by inviting them to take the time to look deep within and exploring their inner world.

The inner world

Human beings have an inner and an outer world, an ability to focus our attention from what is occurring outside of us to what we are experiencing inside. We can also change our experience of the outside world with our intent, as when we daydream, thereby creating an 'altered state' from our normal waking way of being.

To navigate our speedy, chaotic world successfully and peacefully, we need to make space for quiet time and relaxation. I believe relaxation and silence nurture the development of a healthy inner world where children can alter their own states of awareness, without drugs or alcohol. Quiet time allows children to use their creative imagination and can be encouraged at home or in the classroom. It is best to start the practice from an early age and to continue to nurture it through to the final years of schooling and beyond as a lifelong practice of nurturing the inner world. This also provides the foundation for teaching effective stress management for later life. Professor Susan Greenfield in her book *ID: the quest for meaning* writes of her concerns that children no longer have quiet times and stillness to think, ponder and reflect on experiences and life.

> Information technology, nanotechnology and biotechnology are already transforming our lives and they will be pervasive and invasive in unprecedented ways. Now we have a way of subsuming individual identity, or perhaps a false persona or maybe even of losing one's identity altogether.

Greenfield says because most children in the modern world are doing the same screen-based activities, their brains are being wired the same and we will have a generation of children incapable of original thought, creativity and a search for deeper meaning.

One of the best ways to nurture connection with the inner world is to help children learn how to still themselves and practise deep relaxation techniques.

Relaxation and stillness

Relaxation and stillness exercises can include focusing on the breath, guided visualisations, listening to gentle music or stretching and muscle relaxation. They can be done at home or in the classroom. In a classroom they have so many benefits including helping students to become alert and focused, as well as fostering a more harmonious learning environment. They can also foster a more harmonious inner environment for a child or teenager.

Teenage years are a time when our fledgling adults spread their wings and sample life's many experiences. Teenagers often live with a strong inner critic and the voice of judgement within their heads as they compare themselves to others and life's expectations of them. Being able to reach a deep place of inner calmness and stillness can help them feel better about themselves. Deep relaxation quietens the inner voices. Very deep relaxation combined with deep breathing can create an altered state of awareness that feels 'out of the ordinary'.

Deep relaxation is a simple and gentle way to transcend the normal mundane life of study, school and complex social relationships. Simple techniques such as deep breathing and muscle relaxation exercises allow more oxygen to enter the body, benefiting general wellbeing and body functions. I use these techniques in managing my own life and work and my sons too, have found them powerful in improving their lives and even university study results.

If we allowed more silence and stillness in our homes and schools, our children would ponder more, think more and question more for themselves. Stillness and space allows them to develop and practise 'mindfulness'. Children practising mindfulness pay attention to their whole selves, that is, how they feel, sense and intuit their own 'beingness' in the present moment.

Mindfulness

Although mindfulness is an abstract concept, it is well described here:

> Mindfulness is an open awareness that can be brought to each moment and activity of life. This practice involves the discipline of staying grounded in the present moment, in the here and now, so that the mind does not run to the past or the future. The mind rests in the stillness of the moment as if it were an eternal moment. (Mathes Cane & Duennes 2005)

Encouraging children to practise mindfulness offers them many benefits including that it helps children to:

- come to know themselves and develop a better awareness of themself with compassion and honesty
- pay attention and be in touch with their feelings and assess their current state without judgement
- stop scaring themselves with the endless chatter of the ego-voice and things that are seldom real outside of their minds
- build relationships with their world on their terms
- be authentic and honour their own sacredness
- be aware of their strengths and weaknesses
- make decisions, think independently and creatively and be effective problem solvers
- tune into their inner compass or intuition
- not allow others to control them and not control other people
- have a sense of truth that causes them to react when a story doesn't quite 'add up'
- focus their thoughts on an objective, while tuning out distractions
- build psychological strength and avoid depression
- develop personal authenticity and reduce selfishness.

Given mindfulness offers children so many benefits it is important to help them develop the ability and make time to practise. This begins with helping children to know what it is to be present by focusing on and slowing down their breathing, their body and their mind. From this place of stillness and quiet, parents and teachers can encourage children to:

- practise thinking deeply by considering questions and problems which require the development of reasons and explanations, a consideration of alternatives and an assessment of pros and cons
- ponder on a variety of areas including: personal topics like – do you focus on your appearance or who you are; ethical dilemmas such as is it right to tell a lie when you know it may hurt someone's feelings; or qualities like what makes a person brave?

- regularly engage in reflection on topics such as how do you feel right now, have you learned anything new today, have your values and beliefs changed over time?
- journal every day – write 'anything' that comes to them or that they feel they would like to share with themselves and write down.

A final note

Our children live in a very different world to the one we grew up in. I firmly believe they need their parents during adolescence now more than ever before. Drug-affected or addicted teenagers can come from any family, any cultural group and any community. I have some very special friends who are loving, caring parents and yet who have a daughter who struggled with a heroin addiction. Don't be complacent or judgemental; be a good role model, be well informed, be involved with your kids and their friends, be present and especially be vigilant. By providing naturally transcendent opportunities for children and teenagers to experience 'highs' we may help reduce the other unhealthy, risky pursuits of the teenage years. Surely it's worth a go.

We can all open ourselves to the magic of silence and stillness. Then we can teach it to our children so they too can take it out into the world and into adulthood as a skill that sustains them during life's challenges. If we do this, they will have more hope, optimism and enthusiasm, and our world can be a better place than it is now.

I'd like to end on my three top tips for parents to soothe our children's world – the three Ss:

1. *Slow down* – walk slower, talk slower, do less, avoid being hurried by allowing an extra 15 minutes than you think you need to get children ready. Ask what you can take out of your life so you can be a calmer parent, especially in the early years – avoid wearing too many hats when your children are young. If you are comfortable and quiet yourself you will model this behaviour for your children.

2. *Soothe more* – remember that brain chemicals flood our children's brains quite irrationally and chaotically. Reassure children they are valued, safe and that mistakes and accidents are normal. Play

soothing music and use aromatherapy burners in the home. Use quiet voices, gentle tones and avoid pressuring your children or initiating significant changes. Massage and safe touch also have calming effects.

3. *Safe space* – is your home child friendly? Can your children relax in a quiet and safe space? Create a safe home environment with boundaries and routines. Have times where mobiles and computers are turned off (like when everyone is supposed to be asleep). Help children learn how to be still, quiet and just 'be' to fill up their energy cup. Ensure children have a good night's sleep. Finally, connect children with nature often.

If everyone made these changes – imagine how different our lives and our world would be.

Further readings

Dent M (2010). *Saving our adolescents: supporting today's adolescents on the bumpy ride to adulthood*. Murwillumbah, NSW: Pennington Publications.

Dent M (2008). *Real kids in an unreal world: building resilience and self-esteem in today's children*. Murwillumbah, NSW: Pennington Publications.

Dent M (2005). *Nurturing kids' hearts and souls: building emotional, social and spiritual competency*. Dunsborough, WA: Pennington Publications.

Greenfield, Susan (2008). *ID: the quest for meaning in the 21st century*. London: Sceptre.

Kessler R (2000). *The soul of education: helping students find connection, compassion and character at school*. Alexandria, VA: Association for Supervision & Curriculum Development Publications.

Louve R (2008). *Last child in the woods: saving our children from nature-deficit disorder*. Chapel Hill, North Caroline: Alongquin Books.

Mathes Cane P & Duennes M (2005). *Capacitar for kids: a multicultural wellness program for children, schools and families*. Santa Cruz, California: Capacitar International.

Siegel D J (2010). *Mindsight: the new science of personal transformation*. New York: Random House.

Sunderland M (2007). *The science of parenting: how today's brain research can help you raise happy, emotionally balanced children*. New York: DK Publishing.

8

Helping children develop a positive relationship with life

Dr Rosina McAlpine based on an interview with Dr Joe Dispenza

Wouldn't it be absolutely wonderful if you knew that your child had the motivation and the skills to achieve their dreams and live life to the fullest? How amazing would it be for your child to know this as a child and to experience it throughout their days?

I realised that this was possible a few years ago, after attending a lecture given by Dr Joe Dispenza where he shared an inspiring story about his daughter and her amazing relationship with life. He explained how she had made many of her dreams a reality. In particular, he shared a story about how his daughter always wanted to experience a shopping spree – you know where she could go into a store, not worry about money and simply have all of the things her heart desired. This is almost every girl's dream, but how many girls actually get to do it? Well, she did it – her dream came true! Dispenza's daughter and her friend were given a shopping spree to the value of US$10,000! Dispenza also discussed how she achieved this. He explained that when his children were growing up he supported them to understand their relationship with the world, discover that they could achieve their dreams and showed them how to go about doing just that!

This was a life changing moment for me and it became my wish for our son. The content of this chapter is based on an interview I conducted with Dispenza not long after that lecture where he explained how he helped his children to achieve their goals and live their dreams. In Dispenza's chapter on emotional intelligence, four of the five dimensions of emotional intelligence were discussed. The final dimension – motivating oneself is discussed in this chapter. Motivating oneself is about being able to work towards a goal and then finding the flow to achieve outstanding performance. In the interview, Dispenza shared the many activities he's used to help his children become motivated and develop the skills they need to achieve their goals. Here's what I learned.

Your children's relationship with life

If your children truly believe that they don't have the power to influence the course of events in their lives and that they can only live the life they're given, then they're unlikely to set goals and attempt to achieve them. That makes sense right? So it's important to help your children develop positive beliefs about their relationship with the world from an early age. It's so empowering for your children to experience their personal power early in life as it brings about a knowing, without a doubt, that in fact they can influence their lives. The ways parents can achieve this is to introduce focused activities that provide opportunities for their children to experience their power. Your children will get the most out of these activities if: they are lots of fun, you work closely with your children, you set age appropriate activities that are achievable and you support their learning throughout the process.

Make it fun

You need to make the activities FUN! If it isn't fun don't do it with your children. If you make children do something they don't want to do, they'll resent and resist it, and won't experience the intended learning benefits. So, only select activities that are fun. Here's a fun exercise Dispenza shared with his children. First he took three slices of bread from the same fresh loaf and placed each one in a separate plastic sandwich bag and sealed them airtight. Then he labelled one HATE, the next was labelled LOVE and the final slice of bread was labelled IGNORE. Each of the sandwich bags was then carefully placed in a different room in the house ensuring they all had similar environmental conditions in terms of light, moisture, temperature etc. He then explained that he'd like to invite *everyone* in the family, mom included, to conduct an experiment together. He explained the nature of the experiment to everyone and enthusiastically pitched it as 'going to be so much fun and really exciting' because they were to be scientists on a journey of discovery to see what influence their words and actions would have on the three pieces of bread. Then, every day the whole family visited each piece of bread to complete the activity together.

Do it together

Initially, when you're teaching your children about their personal power, it is crucial to do it as a family. It's about role modelling, teaching and sharing the whole experience rather than saying 'Have you done your exercise? Why haven't you done it? Now go and do your exercise.' That doesn't sound like much fun and it certainly doesn't sound motivating either.

So, if you'd like to try this bread exercise for five minutes every day for about two–three weeks (or as long as it takes to complete the activity), then your whole family will need to begin by saying hateful and mean things to the bread that is labelled HATE. You could say things like 'I hate you bread, you are the ugliest bread I've ever seen, I can't wait to see you get all mouldy and rotten so I can throw you in the bin, you're useless, tasteless and horrible bread'. Then you'll all move onto the bread with LOVE written on it and, all together say loving and caring words to the bread for five minutes. You could say things like 'you're the best bread I've ever seen, I really love you beautiful bread, you feel like one of the family, we hope you'll always be with us, you're special we feel so lucky to have you in our lives'. The key to this exercise is that everyone says the words with as *much feeling and sincerity* as they can. You all need to give it all you've got for the whole five minutes. You can set a timer to make it more fun. If you role model the behaviour and make it fun, your children will naturally make the most of the opportunity and enjoy the experience. The final piece of bread is never visited, never looked at and never spoken to for the duration of the activity. It is completely ignored.

Make it realistic

If you're not familiar with this activity you may be wondering what it's all about. If you've heard about it then you know that the slice of bread that is cared for with words of love will have the least amount of mould, the bread that has been hated will have more mould and the bread that has been completely ignored will be similar to the hated bread and could have even more mould.

The purpose of this activity is to allow your children to come to understand, through experience, how their actions can affect or influence other things in the world. In this case, by changing their behaviour towards each slice of bread they can influence the rate of growth of mould on the three identical slices of bread. It's crucial that the activity you choose is *realistic* in the sense that it is age appropriate and that your children are capable of *doing* the activity and *observing* their impact. If the task is too difficult and they can't observe their impact, then they're more likely to learn they aren't able to influence their life, which is not what we want for our children. This bread exercise is very helpful as it in the realm of what children can achieve and importantly what they can understand.

This simple bread exercise will provide your young children with experiences that can help them develop a strong foundation to enable them to complete more independent activities later on. However, in the early stages it is especially important for parents to support the learning process.

Support their learning

As the experiment progresses, it's helpful to ask your children to share how they are feeling and if they've noticed any changes. This way you encourage your children to focus their attention on the activity and to reflect, which are important aspects of the learning process. You can ask them to share how it makes them feel inside after they've said five minutes of hateful words as compared with how it makes them feel after they have said five minutes of loving words. It's best to do the activity in that order so you leave your children with a loving rather than a hateful feeling inside.

You can also help them to consider things they may not have thought about on their own by asking questions like, 'Do you realise that we've all been working together every day for two weeks now? Can you see how things have changed slowly over time? Did you notice that at first we didn't see anything happening, but because we didn't give up and kept at it, now there are lots of changes?'

You can then extrapolate this learning to their daily lives by explaining to your children that when they set a goal for something they want to achieve, like getting fit or building a tree house, sometimes they may not see any results at first or only see a little progress. So it's good for them to *expect* little change when they set a goal and are working towards it. It's good to know that if they keep going and don't give up they will eventually, in time and with effort, achieve their goals. Help them to realise that if they quit they will never achieve their goals. The delayed effect of the mould growing in the experiment helps children develop patience and not to expect instant gratification with instant results. It also inspires your children to continue their efforts even if they can't see immediate results. These are wonderful personal attributes and life skills for children to develop. They are very powerful because your children *know* they are true. They discovered them through their actual life experiences by participating in this activity.

You can also make explicit how the actions of the family had a visible impact on the bread. Positive actions like giving love, had a positive effect on the bread, negative actions like being hateful or ignoring the bread had a negative effect. It is then helpful to pose a question for your children to consider. 'If our words, feelings and actions had these obvious effects on the bread, how might your positive or negative words, feelings and actions affect your friends or other people?' Invite them to ponder this question and to share their ideas. They might be able to make the mental leap from this experiment to this situation, and realise that like the bread, their words, feelings and actions can affect people in a positive or negative way.

You may then take it even further and ask something along the lines of 'if your words, feelings and actions affect the bread and they can affect other people, do you think they can also *affect you* in a positive or a negative way?' Invite your children to ponder this question, share their ideas and discuss how they not only impact others but themselves as well. You can ask your children to recall how they felt after five minutes of saying hateful words as compared with five minutes of saying loving words. This will give them a real experience of how it feels.

You can repeat this simple activity a few times to deepen their learning and understanding. For example, the second time you try it might be to repeat and confirm your original findings to ensure that the results weren't simply a chance happening. You might also invite each child to try it by themselves so they can see their own impact on the slices of bread. Subsequently, you can introduce more sophisticated variations of the activity like replacing the bread with planting three seeds, or three small plants and then do the same thing, say hateful words to one, loving words to another and ignore the last, while giving them all the same water, nutrients and other conditions. In this way you allow your children to broaden their experiences by going from the bread, an inanimate object, to a living plant. If your children complete the activity as directed, they will see that in this experiment, the water, nutrients, light etc. were the same and the only thing that varied was *how they acted* towards the plant, it was their behaviour that influenced the rate of growth and health of the plant.

Over time, your children will develop the knowledge and understanding that they can influence themselves and the world around them in either a positive or negative way. They can then extrapolate and come to the realisation that they have personal power and a positive relationship with life. Wouldn't you love to hear your child come to the following realisation?

> If I can affect the bread, the seed, the plant and myself through my feelings, words and actions then I must be able influence other things as well. I must be able to achieve my goals and my dreams.

Dispenza said to never worry about my son in relation to his ability to create his world because

> children are way better creators than their parents will ever be, that is until the moment their parents are enlightened, because children get

it. Children don't analyse or try to figure out where it's going to come from and how it's going to happen as children live in the moment. Adults are always analysing the future, criticising the past and they're rarely in the moment which is where the creative process happens.

As your children mature, the activities you introduce to enable them to experience their personal power need to become more challenging. In this way, the activities match their increasing capabilities and confidence levels. In the early days, you can help them understand how they can discover their goals, set clear intentions and achieve their dreams. Eventually however, parents can allow their children to get on with the creative process themselves and offer support only as it's requested. Dispenza said that his children are all young adults now which means they are old enough to be self-reflective when their creative processes aren't coming to fruition as fast as they'd like them to. The conversations he now has with his children are mainly about what emotion might be standing in the way of them achieving their goals. For example let's say they're spending a lot of time worrying or frustrated about something then Dispenza reminds them that worry isn't going to create a great future! He explains that they need to empty themselves of these emotions to be able to focus their intention on what they want to achieve!

Processes for consciously creating your life

According to Dispenza there are some important processes our children need to learn and personal qualities that they need to develop that support them to consciously create their lives. These include knowing they can create, setting a clear intention, stillness, focus, being in the moment in joy, tenacity and resilience, taking actions as opportunities arise and most importantly, children need to understand that it is who they are *being* that makes dreams a reality.

Knowing I can create my world

The exercises described above using the slices of bread and plants, can support your children to *realise* their personal power by experiencing their influence on the world around them. This is a powerful starting point and provides children with the motivation to go for their dreams. The next step is to be clear about the goals they want to achieve.

Setting clear intentions

You can inspire your children to discover what goals or dreams they'd like to achieve and then help them to get clarity around these goals. For example if your teenager said, 'I'd love to be a famous musician!' Well that's great; however it doesn't embody sufficient clarity to be an achievable goal. To support your child to get clarity, ask questions to elicit more details. For example you could ask 'what instrument or instruments? What kind of music? Solo or in a band? Concerts or recorded music or both?' and so on. Get as much detail and clarity around the goal as you can.

It is also important to help your child explore the feelings associated with the goal by inviting them to feel if they really, really love it or if it's just something that could be interesting. The more joy and excitement that naturally exudes from your child the truer the goal is for them and the more likely they are to achieve it. Once there is clarity around the goal and a genuine excitement, the next step is to help your child realise that it is who they are *being* that manifests their dreams into reality.

Who you're being creates your reality

It is important to help your children understand that it's not just their thoughts that create their reality, not is it just their feelings that create their reality; it is who they are *being* that creates their reality. Being is when a person's thoughts and feelings are congruent, that is, working together and aligned. This congruence can have a powerful impact on the world.

To explain further, let's say you really want a holiday and you start day dreaming and imagining how wonderful it would be on holiday in Hawaii. You see yourself lying on the sand, relaxing in the sun and you're getting a feeling in your body of really *being* on a holiday. You notice how relaxed and happy you feel in this moment and your thoughts and your feelings about having a holiday are congruent so it's like experiencing the holiday. In this moment in time, you are *being* like you would *be* on an actual holiday! By having this imaginary experience in your mind and body often enough, for an extended period of time, you are likely to attract that experience into your life.

On the other hand, let's say you really want a holiday and as you take the time to imagine how wonderful it would be on the sand and relaxing in the sun, you notice that you're actually feeling guilty about taking a holiday because it would cost so much money and you don't have the money. Can you see that your thoughts and your feelings are NOT congruent right now? Your mind is on the wonderful relaxing holiday and your feelings are on the amount of money it would cost. This is not at all like experiencing the wonderful relaxing holiday described in the example above. In this moment in time, you are not *being* like you would *be* on the actual holiday. Your thoughts and feelings are incongruent and soon enough that lovely holiday becomes a regret and you're unlikely to want to attract that experience into your life. Now that you know what it means to *be* what you want to see in your life, how can parents support their children to *be* their dreams?

Being in the moment: stillness, focus and experiencing joy

A key way to help children *be* their dreams is to show them how to take time out every day to sit in stillness and focus on what it is they want to achieve. It's also important to be a role model for them. Dispenza's children would regularly see their father in meditative practices in their home for hours on end. This was considered to be normal in their home.

Initially, it's supportive for children to practise with their eyes closed to avoid distractions. Most importantly, as they're doing the exercise, children need to *experience* the joy of living as if the dream has already been achieved. To illustrate, if we go back to the previous example of the teenager becoming a famous musician, a parent could invite their child to sit in a quiet space where they won't be disturbed and help them to focus with their mind and their heart on what it would be like to be on stage as the lead guitarist in a famous rock band. The child needs to imagine and to feel as if she is *actually experiencing it* right in this moment. She can hear and see the 20,000 fans screaming and cheering, feel the electricity going through her body as she plays the guitar, notice the perspiration trickling down her back and face, experience her happiness and fulfilment and know that if she felt even a tiny bit more joy she'd simply burst out of her skin. She sees herself playing the lead guitar break in the song as it's building and building until it comes to a peak and the singing starts as the crowd goes crazy in admiration of her playing. She's in awe of the whole experience – basking in this joyful state of *being* for as long as it is lasts.

Now this girl is *being* her dream. Her thoughts and her feelings are aligned. When she leaves her mediation she feels different. She *is* a rock star in her mind and her body even though she is not yet a rock star in the world. Obviously this takes practice. If your children grow up practising these exercises, over time and with your help and guidance, they will master them.

The doing part of achieving goals

Your child *being* their dream is a crucial step in the process, however it's not enough. Right alongside doing these *being* exercises every day, your child needs to actually take steps in the world towards making their dream happen. For example, our girl rock star needs to pick up a guitar and practise, practise, practise! In this way she's taking all the necessary steps to achieve her goal. She is working inwardly and outwardly in the world. This is powerful, and in time opportunities will turn up. For example, she may be offered a chance to replace a lead guitarist for a night in a local band. She now has her first gig, and she sees this as a sign that her dream is becoming a reality. Now she is one step closer to it and it's so exciting that it motivates her to keep up her inner and outer practises. But what will she do if something comes up that stands in the way of her achieving her dream?

Tenacity and resilience

The last step in the process of creating, is to support your child to keep up their *being exercises* and their *doing activities* in the world. For guitar girl it would be to keep up both her physical guitar practice and her meditative practices. It's also crucial to help your children to: find the courage and resilience when setbacks come to challenge their resolve; not to quit and to follow their dream no matter what! You can mentor your children until they are strong enough on their own so that they won't let obstacles stand in their way. Help your children stay focused until the day their dream comes true!

Other 'stuff'

There are so many other things that can support your children achieve their dreams. For example they can talk about their dreams with others. This helps them generate the feelings of *being* the dream by getting all excited and joyful while they share their dreams with other supportive people. It's helpful to explain to your children that they should avoid sharing their goals with people who will put them down, ridicule their ideas or be negative in any way about the future achievement of their goals.

As discussed in a later chapter, you can also encourage your children to create vision boards, to go out and see the people who are actually living their dreams and put themselves in their shoes. Most importantly, you can help your children to understand that they mustn't see the vision board as representing something that they don't have, as it would mean that they are *being* in lack rather than *being* their dream. Dreams are not achieved from lack or from wishing or from thinking about them but from *being* them right now in mind and heart even if they haven't yet manifested in the world.

Dispenza says that our current life is a reflection of who we are *being*, so if we create the neural pathways in our brain of already being our dream this will in turn *be* our external reality. I know this sounds complex and possibly even implausible, however, he can back his ideas up with scientific evidence in his book *Evolve your brain* (2007). Dispenza has helped many men and women around the world to make real changes in their lives and live their potential. There are many people who have succeeded in achieving big dreams. Sandy Forster's powerful welfare-to-millionaire story in the following chapter is one such example, Susan Boyle is another.

Susan started singing at 12 years of age and had a dream to be a famous singer one day. Susan decided to enter Britain's Got Talent and for her audition she chose to sing 'I dreamed a dream' from *Les*

Misérables. If you've ever seen the video[1] of her audition you'd know that the judges and the audience didn't even take her seriously, until she began to sing. Now, that audition has been viewed by over 63 million people across the world and Susan rocketed to international stardom. Her dream came true. She is a very well-known and inspirational singer with her first album selling over four million copies. Susan said in an interview that she'd always had a dream to be a famous singer and has worked many years to achieve it. She's living proof of the power of *being* your dream.

This chapter outlined some of the many insights Joe Dispenza shared with his children as they were growing up about developing their relationship with the world and personal power in life. The activities and learning experiences have supported them to achieve their goals and live happy and fulfilling lives. Dispenza said

> my daughter still amazes me to this day. When it comes to her creations, every time she gets clear on what she wants it happens. She's amazing! I remember asking her one day, 'how do you do it?' She said 'I just live my life as though my prayers have already been answered'. I'm like 'that's a genius answer'. So she's taught me more than anyone else when it comes to creation.

I'd like to end this chapter with an amazing story about Dispenza's daughter, her creative abilities and her positive relationship with life. I hope it is as inspiring for you and your children as it was for me! The story goes like this:

> My daughter is the quintessential creator in my life. She's only 20 years old but she's created so many amazing things. She loves working on something she'd like to create in her life, all of my kids do, and the rule is that I can't help them with their creative processes in any way as they want to create the outcomes on their own – but often times they tell me their plans, what's going on for them and so we talk about it.
>
> My daughter told me about what she'd been planning for her summer break. She wanted to work and to travel around Italy, then to meet

---

1 Available: www.youtube.com/watch?v=RxPZh4AnWyk.

up with some of the friends she made while studying art in Italy and finally she wanted to spend a few weeks at home with us on the ranch. I said that it sounded great and reminded her that she knew what to do to make it happen. She'd need to begin every day by thinking, feeling, being and rehearsing that she has *just had* the most amazing summer of her life doing all of the things she'd spoken about in her plans. She'd need to keep doing her practice until she'd deeply experienced the immense joy of that summer in her mind and body. Then it was OK to get up and go out into the day knowing everything would work itself out and that she didn't need to worry about how or when it might happen. She said 'sure dad no problem'.

Two weeks later she called and said 'OK, here's what's happened. Here's the feedback I'm getting from life about my summer. I can go to Italy and I can take a college course I want to do but it costs $7000 but don't worry I can get it for around $4500 and then I'd have a little time to see my friends but I still need to work and I don't have a job yet, what do you think I should do?'

I told her that she was getting there but that this wasn't it – she had more work to do to create the amazing summer experience she really wanted. In her morning practice sessions, she needed to immerse herself more deeply in the summer experience by thinking in Italian, feeling Italian and being Italian to create it neurologically and chemically in her body. As usual she said 'OK dad, no problem.'

Not long after that she calls me up so excited and I can't tell if she's laughing or crying to tell me that the most amazing thing has happened. She said 'I did exactly as you said, I've been focussed, inspired and living in the joy of my Italian summer. I started just being Italian again, like I was in Italy again. So I was in the library and the Italian language instructor for the university is talking to my art history instructor and they're having this great conversation in Italian and we all end up talking. The very next day I get a call from the university and they offer me a job teaching Italian as the Italian instructor's assistant and, get this, we'll be travelling around Italy in five different cities for five weeks and at the end I get to spend time in Florence to meet up with my friends!'

So I said 'now that's what you wanted – that's perfect. You've done it again, you're an amazing creator!'

Further reading

Dispenza J (2007). *Evolve your brain: the science of changing your mind.* Deerfield Beach, Florida: Health Communications Inc.

9

Inspiring children to achieve goals

Sandy Forster

Do your children focus their attention on what they would love to achieve or on what they don't want in their lives? If your children experience setbacks, do they give up or rise to the challenge? Do your children see their projects through to the end or are they continually moving on to new things – rarely completing anything they start? The ability to set, stick with and achieve goals will support your children to live successful and fulfilling lives.

This chapter explores how parents can role model, partner with and inspire their children to achieve goals. It all starts with helping your children create clarity around what it is they want to achieve. They are more likely to succeed if the goal is important to them and they can stay motivated and focused on the outcome. Goals don't achieve themselves so effective action towards achieving the goal is an important key for reaching the target. Persistence and resilience are qualities that can help children continue towards making their dreams come true despite set backs or difficulties on the way.

Goals are not always about achieving dreams. Sometimes, they're about turning hardship into success. For example, if your child is experiencing a difficulty in their life, understanding the source of the difficulty will help them to realise how to overcome it. Whether the goal is about realising a dream or simply overcoming a difficulty – being able to set and achieve clear goals empowers your child to turn a negative situation into a positive one and make their ideas, inspirations and dreams a reality. I have firsthand experience of turning my life of financial hardship around and achieving my dream of financial freedom. In this chapter I'll share the steps that helped me achieve my financial dreams. You can use these principles to help your children achieve their goals.

My goal

When I was 16 I met a boy, fell in love and 11 years later we got married. My son was just six months old and my daughter was three when we divorced. From that point on, I spent many years struggling to make ends meet. It seemed that no matter what I did, when it came to money, I was always broke and that was the enormous difficulty I had to overcome. Money, or should I say the lack of money, frustrated me, scared me and had me worrying about what the future might hold for me and my children.

After many years of financial hardship, I eventually discovered a way out. I embraced and applied it on a daily basis – it was the catalyst for transforming my family's world. My goal was to go from being on welfare to being a millionaire and … I succeeded!

You might be thinking, well that can't apply to everyone, and if that's what you believe or if it's not a goal that you or your children desire, then of course you won't complete the necessary actions to make it a reality. That's why a person's beliefs and where they focus their attention will either support or hinder them in achieving goals.

Focus and intention

You may believe your children don't listen to a word you say, but you'd be surprised at what sinks in when you think they're ignoring you. I'm continually telling my children, 'What you focus on becomes your reality.' When I was in the very early stages of finding financial security, money was coming in but it was also going out just as fast! I recall my daughter saying, 'Blah blah blah. We don't need a lecture about that focus and create your reality stuff because it doesn't work anyway – we've still got no money!'

That was the truth. We were still struggling financially even though I was clearly focused on my goal of being a millionaire. A few times every day I would say positive affirmations and I would visualise scenes in my mind where I had lots of money. These practices helped me to stay focused on the goal. However, what I wasn't seeing was that for the rest of the day my attention was on the bills. Every time I thought about the bills I experienced fear, worry and panic about where the money would come from to pay for them. That meant that most of the time my focus was on not having enough and believing that I'd be struggling forever.

You've probably heard of the expression 'out of the mouths of babes'. Well, this applies to me as it was in fact my daughter who alerted me to what I was really focusing on and the lack I was creating in my life. It happened when my daughter was around 12 years old. She asked me for some new clothes and shoes for her school dance which was on the very next day.

To provide some context – I'd had a very bad week financially. One of my cheques bounced, a few bills had come in, including a red-letter bill (you know those scary ones with the overdue notice threatening to cut off the supply), and I was beginning to go into my usual feelings of panic about money. The conversation with my daughter went something like this:

'Mum, can you buy me clothes and shoes for the dance tomorrow, I really need them?'

'Darling, I don't have the money right now.'

'You never buy me anything and *I have to have* them!'

'Darling, I'm sorry but I just don't have the money.'

'Can't you just put it on your credit card?'

The credit card was charged to the limit, so that wasn't an option. At this point in the conversation I started to freak out. I was seething with all sorts of very strong, negative emotions. Frustration, because even though I was making good money, it was disappearing; embarrassment, because I felt so hopeless at managing my money; guilt, because I felt like a bad mother for not being able to buy things for her; sadness, because I knew how disappointed she would be because she'd be missing out once again and anger, because she was asking me for something I just couldn't give her.

Unfortunately, of all the emotions I was feeling my anger won, and the conversation was not pretty. The veins on my temples were throbbing, my eyes were bulging out of their sockets, I was hissing through gritted teeth, I had spit flying out of my mouth and I'm sure there were traces of steam coming out of my ears as I screamed like a banshee going to war:

> 'I don't have the money to pay all our bills; I've got to try and pay the phone bill before they cut the phone off. We just don't have the money – don't you understand; we're broke right now – WE … DON'T … HAVE … ANY … MONEY!!!!'

Then she looked me squarely in the eye and with all of the wisdom from her 12 years upon this earth she said to me in her most disgusted tone:

> 'Well if that's how you FEEL whenever you think about money – we're NEVER going to be rich!'

I felt like someone had just punched me in the stomach. In that moment, plain as day, I could see why I was still struggling financially. I was attaching my strongest negative emotions to the one thing I *didn't want*. I was focusing all my attention on my lack and pushing money away. I chuckle now, as I thought she hadn't listened to a word I'd said about focus and creation in making dreams come true!

My emotional outburst was not about having money; it was about NOT having money. So not having money was my dominant focus every day. You might recall in the earlier chapter on emotional intelligence, Dispenza talked about a study where an equal number of funeral scenes and feast scenes were shown to a group of people who were depressed and to a group of people who were emotionally balanced. The results showed that the people who were depressed tended to focus on the funeral scenes and the people who had a balanced emotional disposition thought there were many more feast scenes. The point is that it's people's emotional states that influence what they see and focus on in the world!

So by changing my focus to my abundance goal and taking my attention off the financial lack I was experiencing, I was able to manage my emotions and stay more balanced. This helped me to be more present, see the many opportunities I'd attracted into my life and enabled me to take action towards creating financial abundance.

Taking action

While it is important to think rich and feel rich it's not enough. In other words, it's also important to take steps towards achieving your goals as the opportunities arise. When helping your children achieve their goals, start small and over time help them see that they can achieve larger life goals and eventually that they can make all their dreams a reality. The exciting part is that you get to use your imagination and your creativity together. Children LOVE to spend time imagining all the things they want in their life, so it's easy to get them involved in creating. This way you can role model and share the joy of the process with them. Here's an example of how I got my children involved during the early days of working towards making my first million! At that time I drove a car I hadn't really looked after, so it was quite a wreck – it was very rusty and leaked. Every time it rained, the water would come in through the roof and sit in puddles on the floor so the car would have that really musty, mouldy smell about it. This was particularly problematic as I live on the Sunshine Coast in tropical Queensland in Australia and when it rains, it really pours!

One day after a particularly heavy rainfall, my children, Danielle 12 and Dane nine were getting into the car to go to school and Dane said, 'Mum, there's a plant growing in the back of the car.' Sure enough, a seed must have been brought in on one of the kids' shoes and with all that water; a small tree had sprouted overnight. It was already about 15 cm high!

It was then I realised that we really needed a new car – but I had NO money. However, with my new approach I'd learned that it was important to take steps toward achieving my goal, so I suggested to the kids that we visit some car yards to look for a new car. The kids were so excited which got me even more excited. Doing this together made the energy and the buzz about getting a new car even larger. We'd been experiencing money challenges and going without for so long that we were really looking forward to doing this together. I liked the idea of a 4WD and my friend had a Toyota RAV4, so we went looking in the local car yards for one just like hers.

Once we found a RAV4 that we all liked, we took it for a test drive. I knew how important it was to 'feel' like we already had the car now rather than focusing on what it might be like to have a car in the future. What better way to have that new car feeling than to go and actually experience what it feels like to drive a NEW car!

After the test drive we were all feeling so excited talking about having a 'brand new RAV4'. While driving home my daughter saw a Land Rover car yard and said we should stop for a quick look. Once she saw the Land Rover she decided we should look no further – we simply had to get the new Land Rover Freelander. I jokingly call my daughter a princess as she only wants the best of everything in life! Well, who was I to argue – it really looked great. One tiny problem – the car was $35,000 and I had NO money, was $100,000 in debt and at this point, only bringing in around $18,000 a year!

Ignoring all of that – we took the Freelander for a test drive. We then had a photo taken of the kids and I draped over the car so we could put it up on the wall at home where we could all see it. This way we could look at it regularly to help us keep our focus on the new car and motivate and inspire us to achieve our goal! The power of pictures should never be underestimated.

Creating a vision board

Helping your children develop a clear picture of what they want can help them achieve their goals. A vision board is a great way to help them focus on their goal and it's a creative and fun activity too! My children and I have created many over the years. To help your children create a vision board you need to do some preparation. You'll need:

- a large piece of cardboard or a board (wood, cork, white) for each child

- one or more individual photos of each child – with very happy faces!
- a variety of new or old magazines with lots of colourful pictures in them
- scissors, glue, coloured pencils, coloured marker pens, stickers etc.

You don't need to spend a lot of money on new magazines – recycled magazines are great. Simply ask your friends or the receptionist at your local doctor, dentist or other health professional for their old magazines. Then ask your children if they have a dream or goal they'd like to achieve. It might be to make more friends, be more successful at school, feel calmer, learn the guitar, have a bike or electronic gadget of some sort or improve their fitness. It's good to start with something that is age appropriate and achievable – so encourage them to tell you about a few of their goals. It's also fine if they don't really have a clear goal in mind as the activity can still be completed.

Invite your children to do some craft with you to create their very own special vision board. Explain that a vision board can help them see their goal clearly and that it's easier to achieve a goal if they know exactly what it is they want to achieve. The vision board can also help keep them focused on their goal and inspire them to discover the actions they need to take to achieve the goal. Seeing their goal on the vision board every day brings about feelings of excitement and provides motivation for completing the actions too! Explain to your children that there are a number of steps in creating a vision board and that it can take hours or days or even a few weeks depending on how much time and effort they put into creating it.

Step 1

Give your children a pile of magazines with colourful pictures. If they have a goal in mind, ask them to go through the magazines and cut out pictures or words that are relevant for their goal. For example, if your child's goal is to make more friends then she can cut out pictures of groups of young children playing together, or if she'd like to join a sports team, pictures of children playing that sport. It's also good to cut out headline words and letters to make words like 'friends are forever' or 'basketball is fun'. Pictures of flowers, hearts, butterflies and any other things that make her smile are great too!

If your child doesn't have a clear goal then ask them to find pictures that make them feel happy or represent goals they may aspire to in the future – like becoming a doctor or a zookeeper. Your children will need time to do this. Going through the magazines can be quite time consuming as the aim is to find just the right pictures and words. Ask them not to rush, and to have fun picking great pictures and using their imagination. You may like to help them for a while until you can see they have the right idea. After they've been through the magazines they should have quite a good pile of pictures and words ready for step 3.

Step 2

Ask your child to place one of their photographs right in the middle of the board – this makes it their personal vision board and their goal! They can also place other photos of themselves on the board if they want.

Step 3

Ask your child to look through the pictures and the words they've cut out and to select their favourites. Next ask them to arrange the pictures and words on the board (but no glue yet). The aim is to have fun, to really connect with their goal and to be creative while arranging the pictures and photos. Explain that they should spend as much time as they need arranging everything until it *looks* and *feels* right. For example, they might start by arranging some words that are inspiring and relevant to their goal like: success, friendship, fun, calm, power or health. Or they may simply choose to arrange the pictures on the board around their photograph in the centre. Once your child is happy with the placement of the pictures and words – they can go to step 4. Your children can discard any pictures or words that they don't want during the process or keep them for another vision board.

Step 4

Once the final layout is prepared its time to glue everything onto the board. Invite your child to be creative by adding handwritten words, colour with pencils, paint or markers, their own drawings, stickers or glitter etc. They can use the vision board to create a work of art to inspire them to achieve their goal!

Step 5

Find a special place for the vision board – somewhere your child will see it and be inspired by it. It could be in their bedroom or the family room, and it's good if you can ask your child where they'd like it to be.

Now coming back to our story – we used the photo of the kids and I draped over the car to motivate us and stay focused on our goal! Because we saw it every day we talked about it together and got excited about our new car. We knew we would have that car one day; we knew it would be ours. While looking at our picture we could remember how great it felt to have a new car, how it smelt and we talked about how people would look at us when we were in it – as you can imagine the kids were quite embarrassed about being seen in our *old* car. Whenever I looked at the picture of the car it inspired a great feeling of certainty in me – I'd have that car – I could feel it in my bones even though I had NO money right now.

With my new focus on abundance, during the next six months many money-making opportunities came my way. I had the intention and the motivation to take the actions needed. I tried many different activities to make money with some more successful than others. However, despite any setbacks I encountered, I remained focused and persistent. Eventually my persistence paid off and one thing led to another and before I knew it I was down at the Land Rover yard, picking up our new silver Freelander. When the lady handed over the keys to my new car she said:

'I bet you're excited.'

'Excited? You have no idea how excited I am. Six months ago I was on welfare with over $100,000 in debt and here I am picking up my new Freelander. I've just moved into a beautiful house on the water and I'm about to go to an amazing personal development seminar – the new business I've started which is making lots of money. Yes, I'm REALLY excited.'

Believe me, the kids and I were thrilled to bits. We had smiles from ear to ear as I drove our new Freelander out of that car yard.

Persistence

Have you had a time where everything is going really well and you're on track for achieving your goal and then, out of the blue there's a setback or worse still everything seems to be going against you? I certainly experienced my fair share of setbacks and bumps in the road on my journey to financial freedom. For example, I had imported these great slippers from China that could help reduce back pain by aligning the spine. They definitely worked as I tried them myself so I knew their benefits.

Feeling inspired and confident that everyone with back pain would like to be pain free using this simple solution – I imported a whole container of slippers, set up a website to sell them online and organised for a TV station to do a story on them. I was so excited – this was my chance to get rich and make my first million! However, there were many setbacks. For example, my story got moved forward week after week. On the night it finally went to air it followed a story on the tragic Bali bombings! Now who in their right mind would be interested in buying slippers when people had died? I only made 12 sales and I was completely distraught! I expected thousands of orders and it had all gone awry.

I cried for days, I was so upset, I felt despondent – who wouldn't? But nevertheless, after I calmed down, I kept on going. Well let's face it, I'd never make a million dollars if I gave up! On my journey to achieving my goal, I've learned many things including that setbacks and difficulties are a part of life and, if you let them, they will help build your tenacity and resilience. I know it was my unwavering belief that I would become financially free one day, my constant focus on my goal, and most importantly, all of the efforts I made when opportunities to earn money opened up which actually lead me to where I am today – a millionaire! One way to support a child's persistence is to count and reward their progress and achievements in relation to the goal.

Counting achievements – no matter how small

Sometimes goals take days, weeks or even years to complete. The longer they take, the more effort is needed to stay on track and keep going towards achieving the goal. Help your child understand that one way to stay motivated is to recognise and count achievements – even the really small ones. Counting and recognising each task they've completed helps your children realise they are now one step closer to achieving the goal and so they are more likely to be motivated to keep going. For example, if a child has a goal to lose weight, if every time that child loses some weight, no matter how small, they recognise and acknowledge their achievement then they will more likely be motivated to keep going towards their weight-loss goal. Counting every weight loss shows progress and inspires further action. Alternatively, if your child has lost no weight, they can count how many days they have been on the diet and doing exercise. In this way they can count the effort and acknowledge that it will eventually reap rewards.

It is most important that your child counts their own achievements rather than relying on others. This will support the development of a strong sense of self and resilience. This can be done by having an action list to tick off for effort or for outcomes which clearly shows progress. Encourage positive self-talk like 'yes! I'm getting there. Well done to me as I have completed one more thing on the list and so if I keep going it won't be long before I reach my goal.'

You can also encourage your children to reward themselves sometimes for doing really well. For example if they have spent three hours working on homework, they could reward that achievement by taking a 15-minute break and playing a computer game they love! It can also be helpful to share their progress with you or others who are supportive of them – only if they count, recognise and cheer their achievement. Don't encourage sharing with people who won't support their progress, and it's more important that your child values their own achievement anyway!

Concluding comments

Supporting your children to learn how to achieve their goals will help them lead successful and fulfilling lives. You can invite your children to develop their imaginative skills and to discover what inspires them. It's important to help them get a clear idea of what it is they want so they can focus their attention and energy on the goal rather than focusing on the difficulty or lack they are currently experiencing. This will help them to see and take advantage of the opportunities that open up for them to complete actions towards achieving their dreams. Don't let setbacks stop them in their tracks but inspire them to keep going and enjoy the exciting outcomes that arise from a positive attitude and persistence!

I believe the most important thing you can do for your children is to be a great role model. If you show them what can be done by believing in yourself, staying focused on your goal, never giving up when obstacles come your way and taking actions whenever opportunities arrive – you will achieve your goals. This will inspire your children to achieve their dreams too. The second most important thing is to work on goals together with your children until they're ready to do it on their own.

So, if it worked for our family it can work for you too. What could you and your family co-create if you put your minds and hearts to it?

Further reading

Forster S (2004). *How to be wildly wealthy fast: a powerful step-by-step guide to attract prosperity and abundance in your life today.* Mooloolaba, Qld: Universal Prosperity.

10

Learning partnerships with children

Dr Yvonne Sum

The word 'parenting' can bring up a variety of feelings and memories for different people. We've all experienced being parented when we were children – whether it was with our biological parents or with foster/ adoptive carers. When you reflect on your childhood, in general, do you have fond memories of the parenting style you experienced or not?

If you don't have children, you can probably imagine that your experiences during childhood might have a profound influence on your parenting style when you do have children. If you are a parent, you might have already experienced that for yourself when you heard your mother's or father's words automatically come out of your mouth. Furthermore, if you hated how you were parented, with your child you might have chosen to do the exact opposite of what your parents did with you. If you loved your childhood experiences you might try to model your behaviour on your parents. Whatever the case, your experiences of being parented affect how you parent.

My journey into parenting

My experiences as a child were wonderful. My parents did such an awesome job raising four diversely different personalities and that set a high standard for me to emulate. I wanted to be as good as my parents and that stopped me from becoming a mum for a long time. I thought I could never live up to such high standards. On top of that, my life was great and I didn't want to lose that freedom by having a child or two. I also remember stressing about the question 'how can I bring up another human being when I'm not even sure I can look after myself?'

So, as you can see I was a 'reluctant parent' and falling pregnant brought on antenatal depression. I felt as though my life as I knew it was truly over! Thankfully, soon after Jett, my oldest son was born I had an inspired realisation and accepted a few fundamental ideas that made me feel OK about being a mum:

1. I don't have to have all the answers
2. I don't have to do it exactly as my parents did
3. I can enjoy parenting as a journey filled with positive opportunities for me to learn and grow as a person alongside my child.

My first lesson: parenting is a learning partnership

When Jett was born 12 years ago, I remember spending hours simply absorbed with him. It felt like all my senses opened up and we connected at a deep level. He was the most gorgeous being to me and this made it easy to give him my complete attention. Like so many new parents, I remember thinking I wish Jett came with a 'manual'. It was then I realised, every child *is their own* manual and can guide their parents if the parents are open to *reading the book that is the child.*

As time went on, I experienced more and more how parenting is a learning partnership – I learnt from Jett, he learnt from me and we were growing together. I spent endless hours talking, singing, reading him books, tickling him, helping him with his first steps and watching him reach milestone after milestone with my encouragement. As I reflect back I learnt so much from him too. He inspired me with his tireless efforts to crawl, then pull himself up and then finally take steps – never being deterred by falling, never giving up – but showing a determined effort to master his next skill.

As he grew, I remember the joy of learning about, and seeing the world, through his eyes. The many, many questions – the insatiable curiosity about why the grass is green, the sky blue and why rain pitter patters on the roof. The simplicity of being in the moment together – was yet another example of our growing and changing learning partnership. As time went on my wonderful daughter Xian was born and I had even more to learn. Little by little, as the learning partnership involving my husband and me as well as our children evolved, so did my understanding of parenting and the 7 Rs of Parenting emerged.

The 7 Rs of Parenting?

When Jett turned five and Xian was three, I was invited to give a presentation at the Sarawak Women's Council conference in Malaysia on 'Parenting for now and for the future'. In reviewing and reflecting on my experiences as mum, the child development and parenting material I'd read and the stories I was planning to share with the audience, it became clear that the 'tips' I hoped to share were commonsense essentials that built the foundations of joyful parenting in a loosely structured way. Like the 3 Rs of educational foundations: Reading, 'Riting, 'Rithmetic … I uncovered the 7 Rs of Parenting essentials which is the focus of this chapter. It's the framework I use and have shared with so many families to help them *make it all work!* For me it's a framework or structure for parenting that supports the learning partnership between children and their carers.

The 7 Rs of Parenting is depicted on the following page as a circle – each of the 7 Rs working together as key parts in the parenting process. No matter which one I choose to work on, I find that each one seems to support the others in a variety of ways – and that is how the 7 Rs evolved.

The 7 Rs are introduced in the following sequence, but they can be explored in any order that feels right for you and your family:

1. Role modelling
2. Respect
3. Rules
4. Routine
5. Review and Reflect
6. Reorganise
7. Running it – Response-ability

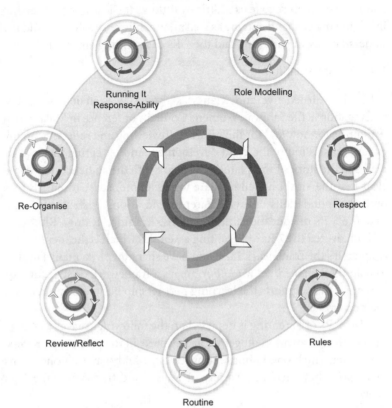

Tribal leadership in action

As I explain each of the Rs from time to time in the text, I invite you to ponder and reflect on how you might already do this with your family or how you might try that particular *R* with your family. This will help you make it both relevant and personalised to you. So let's explore the 7Rs of Parenting principles one by one ... beginning with role modelling.

R#1 – Role modelling

Role modelling is at the heart of parenting and authentic leadership. It is essentially about being an example for your child to learn from and to follow in terms of their behaviours, beliefs and values. Our children need role models to inspire them – someone to look up to and emulate while they find their own way in the world. A parent's behaviour can be said to be the clearest form of communication – we've all heard of the sayings – 'actions speak louder than words' and a leader is expected to 'walk their talk'.

Most parents want to be a good example for their children but it doesn't always work out that way. Sometimes we are not aware of things we have done until we experience our children repeating it back! Role modelling is how our children will learn the most from us – consciously and mostly, unconsciously. Sociologist Morris Massey describes three major periods of child development and the impact of role modelling on them (Massey 1986).

1. *The imprint period* – up to the age of about seven, children are like sponges absorbing ... everything around them and accepting much of it as true, especially when it comes ... from their parents.

2. *The modelling period* – between the ages of eight and 13, children copy people in their environment, most often their parents but other significant people like their teachers as well. Rather than blind acceptance, they are trying things like experimenting with different clothes to see how they feel.

3. *The socialisation period* – between 13 and 21, children are largely influenced by their peers. As they develop as individuals and look for ways to move away from the earlier programming, they naturally turn to people who seem more like them. Other influences during this period include: the media, social networks – especially those aspects which seem to resonate with the values of their peer groups.

Can you think of a time when you've seen your children 'mimicking' you? Your child's behaviour has been *imprinted* from absorbing your actions or *copied* from you as a role model. Have you seen a similar stance, heard your tone of voice and the exact words being used by an older child to a younger sibling? Role modelling as a parent is key to helping your children develop in the formative pre-teen years.

So what are you role modelling? Is it conscious behaviours, values and beliefs or unconscious habits and reactions? I have spent and continue to spend many hours reflecting upon and clarifying who I am as a role model for my children. My aim is to be authentic and live from the behaviours, values and beliefs that support my life and the lives of my children. This is not an easy thing to do and requires constant work and sometimes I get it wrong! When I make a mistake I apologise and explain this to my children – as this is another value I want to role model for my children – to be OK about making mistakes, to have the courage and grace to say sorry, and to see how mistakes provide a person with the opportunity for growth.

One of the most important things I'd like to come back to is that children will *do as you do* and not so much *do as you say*. What you role model is what generally *goes in*. For example, do you make time to care for yourself and relax and rejuvenate, or not? What are you role modelling with this behaviour? Your behaviour is saying that it is not important to relax and take care of yourself but instead it is good to run yourself into the ground and do everything for everyone else. Is that what you'd like your child to emulate and learn?

Being a good role model is about leading a true life that is to me based on my ongoing discovery of who I am, my purpose and living from vision. My hope and legacy is that my children do not become clones of me, but in turn find *their* truth of living a great life. I believe that positive role models engender respect in self and others.

R#2 – Respect

The word respect has so many different meanings today. How often have you heard parents say 'the children of today have no respect – in my day I respected my parents'. What then is the meaning of respect in today's environment?

I was recently thumbing through a few books on parenting and found very little reference to the topic. I could only conjecture two things:

1. Respect is a given assumption in parenting, OR
2. Respect is old hat – and it's not cool to discuss this.

Upon reflection, the meaning of respect in the context of 'the old days' had the connotation of a need to obey, abide by or secede to traditions, authority or an older person. This is a respect gained from the fear of negative consequences. Do you want your child to respect you out of fear or out of love? Fear-based respect is not the kind of respect I am talking about here. Allow me to revitalise and make contemporary the meaning of respect in the context of the 7 Rs.

Respect can be accorded anyone and it is about regarding someone or something with admiration, esteem and reverence as a result of their abilities, qualities or achievements not necessarily because of their title, position or chronological age. This is more about inspiring the child to hold their parents in high esteem as they draw forth the best in themselves and in others. Parents who are respected can act as a wonderful role model for their children.

How can parents invite and nurture this kind of respect from their child? For me it is about building on the first of the 7 Rs by being a good role model to my children and living from respect myself. For example, if I make a promise to my children – I demonstrate my respect for them by keeping my word. I also try and see the world from their perspective and respect them as human beings in their own right. I remember one time Jett asking to go out to play in the rain. My first impulse was to say 'No, you'll catch a cold' but stopped myself and instead asked 'Why would you want to go out and get wet?' He explained that he thought it was like 'having a shower from heaven' and that he would like to try it. Since it was summer and we could run in and have a bath immediately, I agreed to join him. In fact – I took Xian out with me too! I must admit I had so much fun as we ran around in our swimmers in the warm summer downpour! It is mutual respect that is key to the learning partnership my husband and I are nurturing with our children.

In what ways do you respect your child? In what ways do you inspire your child to respect you? Do you model the kind of respect in your home you'd like your children to develop for their own life, for other people and for the environment? These are the key questions that will help you create the learning partnership around developing mutual respect with your child. This leads us into the next one of the 7 Rs.

R#3 – Rules

Like respect – the word 'rules' can have a number of meanings and can invoke a variety of negative feelings about being controlled. However, I believe rules can be seen in a positive light and are an important part of parenting. For example, in sport the rules provide the purpose, structure and directions for the game. The rules help the players understand the aim of the game, how to play it safely and the consequences when rules are broken. There can even be different rules for different players in the game, for example, in soccer the goalkeeper has different set of rules to the striker. Games also need the right setting or environment like a basket ball court and ring for the game of basketball. While rules might be somewhat constraining, they keep the game safe and fun.

Relating these ideas back to the family we can ask the same question – what is the purpose of rules? Similarly to sport, rules set the boundaries and structure by which every family member agrees to behave in different contexts. There are safety rules – e.g. holding hands when crossing the road for young children, driving rules and safe sex rules for young adults. There are rules for helping the household function efficiently, where the chores or jobs are allocated like stacking the dishwasher. What are the rules in your home? Do they make for a safe and fun environment? More to the point is everyone *willing* to play by the rules?

From time to time it is good to look at the rules that are functioning in your home. To do this you can ask questions like:

- What rules have we got in place – spoken and unspoken?
- Are the rules being followed? If not why not?
- Are there any rules that disadvantage some family members and not others?
- Are some rules no longer needed or need to be revised – like curfew or bed times as children get older?
- Have the rules been passed down without reviewing them?
- Have the rules been discussed and created together as part of a learning partnership or have they been imposed?

I'd like to explore in more depth the last point on the importance of a partnering between parents and children in relation to family rules. All rules, whether handed down or newly co-created, need agreement by family members for them to work as intended in the 7 Rs. That is not to say that there may not be rules that your children are unhappy with, but it is important to share with them to help them understand why and how they can be of benefit to the family as a whole.

Some rules have come from traditions handed down over generations and sometimes revision is necessary. There was once a family tradition handed down for over a hundred years and it was to do with Thanksgiving. In this family, every year the Thanksgiving turkey was served with the limbs amputated. One day, a Gen Y grandchild challenged the tradition. She was promptly told that 'We've always done it this way'. Not to be put off, our young investigative journalist revealed that great-great-great-great-great-great grandma had too small an oven – so the limbs had to be removed to cook the turkey![1] The following Thanksgiving, the turkey graced the table with all its limbs intact. Moral of the story: rules that are no longer relevant or useful need to be reworked, revamped or refined.

There are also unconscious ingrained beliefs that rule us, e.g. when a child brings back a maths quiz with a score of 98%, the unconscious rule that looks for 'what did you not get right?' puts our focus on the two percent that was answered incorrectly. How would it be if we consciously refined that rule to a more empowering 'how did you get those 98% right?' We can then positively reinforce what they did well to improve that two percent they missed this time!

Perhaps you can take some time to review the rules you have in your house and come together in a learning partnership with your children to review and create shared and agreed-upon rules, and to uncover disempowering rules. The right rules are great in many ways and they are especially helpful for supporting the family to follow their routine which is the fourth of the 7 Rs.

---

1 See 'Snopes: rumour has it': www.snopes.com/weddings/newlywed/secret.asp.

R#4 – Routine

Routines conjure up reactions that can range from: 'I love routines they help me manage my life' to 'I hate routines they cramp my spontaneity'. How do you feel about routines? Can you imagine a day without any routines? On a positive note, a day without routines would mean being in the unknown and allowing for spontaneity. You could choose to do whatever you wanted, whenever you wanted – all in the moment. This would invite a great scope to experiment but it could result in chaos too. Imagine if there was no routine timetable for the bus or train. Then you could be waiting five minutes or five hours! Whether we like it or not, our lives are governed by routines. A day with routines allows for planning and certainty. Children find certain routines helpful as it gives them structure and certainty whilst ironically supporting freedom.

One of the important benefits of routines for children is that they foster independence and this independence cultivates self-esteem. If children know as soon as they get up they get dressed – over time they will learn the routine and be able to dress themselves. Routines also provide children with security – they know that certain things will run at a certain time and certain people will be in attendance at those times. Routines also decrease the need to communicate as often, so people can show up or do things without being reminded.

As my children mastered their routines they didn't need to keep asking me things and vice versa! They each have a timetable for their daily activities which gives them the autonomy to prepare for their school day or other activities without looking to me. Structured routine gives predictability and empowerment to act without constantly checking with parents. Both Jett and Xian know that their routine is to complete their daily homework and music practice before watching TV or playing computer games. So they know they don't have to ask for permission once they have completed these tasks.

Like rules, routines are best worked out together in a learning partnership. In this way you show your children respect and invite them to contribute which means they are more likely to enjoy and comply with the routine willingly! You also empower them with a skill for life – the ability to develop, review and maintain routines! You can also be flexible and let them set the routines on weekends or school holidays – where the routines might not be as important as week days!

How do you deal with routines in your home? Have the children been involved in their creation? Are there any routines that need reviewing? While routines offer so many benefits we also need to take a break from routines to make time to review and reflect.

R#5 – Review and reflect

The fifth of the 7 Rs of Parenting is review and reflect. In my family we call this 'R&R' time. It is about taking a break from the routine of doing to 'practice the pause'. R&R time creates a space for the family to review and reflect on personal and family matters. It starts by setting aside a regular time to pause, reassess and take stock. This allows all family members to talk about personal and family issues by sharing what's working or not working, to celebrate the successes and to discover new ways to improve how the family supports each other.

R&R is another avenue for nurturing the learning partnership between parents and their children. We regularly take time out as a family and we have a few different kinds of R&R times throughout the year. For example we have the New Year's Resolution R&R where the family comes together to talk about personal and family goals for the year. Then we have the quarterly R&R time for reviewing and reflecting on the day-to-day family *stuff* and finally we have whenever-we-need-to R&R meeting from time to time.

How it works for us

Here's an example of a simple R&R process when conducting our family meetings:

1. *What's hurting?* We generally start by reviewing what's not working and then reflect by brainstorm suggestions of how to do differently. I encourage the children to be grateful for the opportunity for our family to do better and how this helps everyone grow personally. Once the difficulties have all been sorted we then talk about what's working and take time to be grateful and count our blessings.

2. *What's working?* With day-to-day business it is easy to forget to count what's great and sometimes we even discount what we consider to be 'only small wins'. Think back to when your children were tiny and did the simplest things like say mum or grab a toy and you celebrated as if your child had won the Nobel Prize! Helping your child value their own achievements alongside you valuing their achievements, provides positive reinforcement of the behaviour and life skills we want our children to develop.

How does a family make sure they take R&R time? When the children were young, I was responsible for making sure our family had R&R time. Now that our children are older everyone takes turns in calling and facilitating the R&R time meeting (with my help as needed). When I was growing up, a yearly gathering of the family at Chinese New Year created a natural opportunity for my father to initiate the annual R&R. We also had regular family meetings and one of the four daughters took the minutes. We rotated the 'Keeper of the Minutes'. I remember these times fondly. They were times to challenge the status quo to find better solutions as well as talk about and celebrate all of the great things we were doing.

Does your family take time to review and reflect? Can you see the benefit of nurturing this tradition to teach your children life skills, to keep your family working in a happy and harmonious way and to foster the learning partnership between you and your children? Both while growing up and now with my own family, I have experienced the many benefits R&R time can bring. Don't take my word for it, try the R&R time with your family.

Following our R&R time, after we've reviewed, reflected and come up with new ideas to solve the problems we identified, then it's time to put the things into action so we can work in a new way. This brings me to the sixth rule – reorganise.

R#6 – Reorganise

Reorganising is simply the 'doing' that naturally flows on from the R&R 'thinking'. It is about making the necessary adjustments to improve the processes that we all agreed weren't working in our family. For example, the rules we agreed upon as a family about not handling things in stores changed as the kids grew. This is how we progressively reorganised the weekly grocery shopping routine. At two years of age, the kids helped us spot the items on the list as I called it out. At four, they started getting the items within their reach off the shelf (this change was a breakthrough for them). At six, they were given responsibility of holding the list, reading items off it and checking it off. At eight, they helped me work out change at the checkout counter. At 10, they were given a section of the list, we split up to collect our respective items and meet back at the checkout for payment. At 12 they get the grocery shopping done and meet me at another store in the mall where I am running other errands.

Without reorganising things our family would get stuck in the rut of old routines and rules and we wouldn't make the changes that improve our family life. Sometimes the reorganisation doesn't take much and is simply a natural reordering of things – like the shopping routine. At other times, we had to put in a great deal of time and effort – this is what I call a major reorganisation.

Here is an example of a major reorganisation in our family. Up until the children were in junior primary school, my husband and I had been driving them to school on the way to work. The children wanted the freedom to travel by public transport from time to time. My husband and I thought it was a great idea and held a family R&R meeting to work out how we could make this transition. During the meeting I could see that the children needed a gradual but simple way to move from being driven to school, to allowing them to take public transport. Here are the steps we co-created as a result of our meeting:

- Mum takes the bus with Xian & Jett both to and from school for up to a week. On the way, mum points out the train station to Jett who wants to take the train.

- Second week, Jett waits with Xian at the bus stop to put her on the bus before he and mum get on the train. After three trips together with mum, Jett catches the train by himself. Xian comes home by bus with a school friend and walks home with her. Jett comes home by train himself and walks himself home.

- Third week Xian catches bus to and from school by herself. We're in a new routine and we're all happy.

Sometimes our reorganisations are major like when I returned to full-time work (the public transport option above helped the process) but mostly they are little things like getting the children to do more housework as they get older and giving them more independence as to how or when they do their homework. Can you see how having regular R&R meetings to discover the things you may need to Reorganise and then taking the actions needed to make it happen could be of benefit to your family?

These two processes in the 7 Rs of Parenting offer your family a way to continually review and improve the things that are not working well for your family. This brings us to the seventh and final R.

R#7 – Running it: response-ability

Running it: Response-ability is about managing the six principles of the 7 Rs of Parenting we have described above. By response-ability, I mean the ability to respond, not just to be 'responsible' in the traditional sense of the word. Parents have the best intention to be a great role model, to respect their children and to be respected, to have helpful rules, to create routines that enhance family life and to review, reflect and reorganise so there is continuous change and improvement BUT we know that all of this takes time and it won't happen on its own.

Running it: Response-ability is the taking time to plan, schedule and then actually follow the 7 Rs of Parenting principles. This is the engine room stuff. The daily activities of the family. It is a cycle of: actioning – accountability – monitoring – tweaking – actioning ... and so on it goes.

How does your family function? Do you review, reflect and reorganise? For me, Running The 7 Rs of Parenting with response-ability means leading a great life myself and to excite and inspire my family to live a great life. It is about creating an environment where every member of our family can respond to the 'business-as-usual' day-to-day goings-on, as well as the unusual unforeseen that get thrown our way. After all, we live in a world of continuous change.

Our family processes, our learning partnership and our experiences help our children to become more response-able as well. This will set them up with valuable life skills. For instance, I valued my independence as my parents 'slowly released the apron strings' – giving us more and more response-ability as we grew up. In order to nurture that in Jett and Xian, I give them this same opportunity. For example, they can choose to keep their own bedroom tidy or not. I have agreed not go in to clean or tidy. So if they need anything in their mess, they need to find it themselves. They also make their own lunches for school. So if they forget, they either go hungry or pay for their lunch from their own pocket money.

So what are you doing about Running It? How are you response-able to your changing circumstances?

A final note

I sincerely hope you have found my discussion of the 7 Rs of Parenting principles and the stories I shared about my family's experiences helpful. If you'd like to apply the principles of the 7 Rs of Parenting in your family life, my suggestion is that you introduce them one at a time so it is not overwhelming. First choose which of the 7 Rs resonates with you most. Then, plan how you'd like to try it, schedule it into your diary and most importantly do it! Don't worry about how well you will or won't do it – just dive in and give it a go. Most importantly engage your children in the process so you can nurture a learning partnership which will enable you to learn from each other, deepen your understanding of each other, solidify a loving relationship based on respect, grow together and enjoy a happy life.

Further resources

Massey, M (1986). *The Massey triad*. DVD. Enterprise Media, USA.

Index